The Rainbow Machine

Tales from a Neurolinguist's Journal

by
Andrew T. Austin

"A picture held us captive.
And we could not get outside of it,
for it lay in our language
and language seemed to repeat it to us inexorably."
—Ludwig Wittgenstein

Copyright © 2007
All rights reserved
Real People Press
1221 Left Hand Canyon Dr.
Boulder, CO 80302
Website: realpeoplepress.com

ISBN 978-0-911226-44-7 Paperback

Cover art by *Mark Andreas*

Other NLP Books, CDs, & DVDs from Real People Press:
Discover more resources for your personal growth and professional development. A wide range of NLP Books, CDs & DVDs from leading NLP trainers and developers, including:

Heart of the Mind, a unique introduction to NLP that guides you in 20 "life themes." Read actual change sessions, and step-by-step guidelines.

Solutions, a classic introduction to the basic concepts and methods of NLP, with a focus on relationships.

Core Transformation, a ten-step process that uses a limitation as the doorway to profound states many describe as spiritual, such as "presence" "peace" or "oneness. Available as a book and also on DVDs of a complete 3-day workshop.

Six Blind Elephants, a two-volume book that creates a basis for understanding how all change methods rely on three fundamental processes.

CD and *DVD* demonstrations of other methods, including "Resolving Shame" "Eye Movement Integration" "Creating Effective Personal Boundaries" & "Transforming Troublesome Voices."

Visit RealPeoplePress.com for complete list of resources and to order.

The name *Real People Press* indicates our purpose: to publish ideas and methods that someone can use independently or with others to become more real—to further their own growth as a human being and to develop their relationships and communication with others—since 1967.

1 2 3 4 5 6   Printing   11 10 09 08 07

Contents

Introduction

I very seldom recommend books at all, but it is a huge pleasure to recommend this one by Andy Austin, who has one of the brightest minds, warmest hearts, and bravest spirits in the field of Neuro-Linguistic Programming (NLP). Moreover, he uses all these with the utmost skill, creativity, and outrageous playfulness. He is truly a "Lance Armstrong" of NLP; if there were an "extreme games" in NLP working with unusual clients with unique problems, he would win it hands down.

I have to tell you that overall, the wider field of psychotherapy, psychiatry, and personal change—and not a little of the field of NLP—is a shameless shambles—like a *very* dark moonless night that allows you to see very little, and do less, with only a small sprinkling of bright stars, most of whom have extensive training in NLP.

I say this after almost half a century in the field, during which I have experienced thousands of sessions of famous therapists doing therapy with clients, and after spending several decades teaching professionals in trainings, and in presentations at national psychotherapy conferences. Most psychotherapy is ineffective, much of it is harmful, and all of it is expensive. The most common response to this lack of effectiveness is to blame clients for "not being ready to change," and to submerge their problems in drugs that only sweep them under a rug of numbness and lethargy.

In these pages, Andy gives us vivid glimpses of this bleak landscape, but he also shows how rapid and effective therapy and personal change can be when you know what you are doing, and how to do it. Despite 30 years of full-time involvement in NLP, I have learned much from these pages. But don't take my word for it; read a few chapters and find out for yourself.

Steve Andreas

Acknowledgments

This is the bit of the book that anyone who doesn't know me sensibly skips over. It is also the place where I hope I can include everyone I want to thank, which is of course not possible. Should I apologise in advance? Very probably.

Here goes: Thanks to Richard Bandler and John Grinder for their creation of Neuro-Linguistic Programming (NLP), and all those who showed them their stuff. Thanks to Steve Andreas for his guidance in editing this book; to Nick Kemp for his ongoing support and friendship; Perenna Powell for the well-aimed kick up the arse; my parents, Pat and Tim, for their tolerance and eternal patience; David Gould for his unique view on reality; Frank Farrelly for his provocation; Aphra Darlington for her ongoing feedback and The Two Minky's for just being there.

There are lots of others worth a mention. My math teacher at school, Ron Newton, for believing in me and the rest of his class. I should also mention all the Daves, Ali, Corinne, Paul, Darren, Big Bad Al, Andy and Jackie, Alice and Mike for being the best friends a guy can have. And of course I must mention you, the reader, for picking up this book. I sincerely hope you enjoy it.

"I am done with great things and big plans, great institutions and big success. I am for those tiny, invisible, loving, human forces that work from individual to individual, creeping through the crannies of the world like so many rootlets, or like the capillary oozing of water, which, if given time, will rend the hardest monuments of pride."

—William James

Preface

As many travellers to India know, the restaurant menus regularly offer interesting delicacies not before heard of by the visitor. For example, in Hyderabad I came across, *"Chicken Killed In Any Manner of Your Choices."* Essentially what was on offer was a grilled chicken with a choice of sauces, but something critical got lost in translation somewhere. I learned later that "Egg Drop Soup" really *is* a genuine dish but one small eatery I visited probably missed the original recipe—what they gave me was a boiled egg floating in a bowl of hot water. "Well, the English *do* eat the strangest things," was the passing comment from my Indian companion. Mind you, he was still in shock that we ate *cows*, which apparently translates as the culinary equivalent of eating char-grilled puppies.

In Tamil Nadu you may be lucky to chance across a delightful restaurant called, "The Runs," a name that doesn't bode well, but I ate, I enjoyed, and I lived. Meanwhile over in Calcutta there is another place well worth a visit called "Off Cum On Rambo Bar." I was curious—just *what* were they thinking? So in the early afternoon I went in and asked the man standing behind the bar.

"Rambo, yes, good, *yes*?" He made machine gun noises as he pretended to shoot up the place. I thanked him and moved on quickly.

It was the restaurant in Varanasi down by the river that really made my day. Following my delightfully spicy pizza, I found in the pudding section an offering of, *"Plain Bastard"* for just 15 rupees. It was listed next to the ice creams and sorbets.

I ordered it. I *had* to; I'd have paid double just to see what it was.

Ten minutes passed before the waiter returned. "I'm very sorry sir, but plain bastard not possible."

So I asked for it spiced. The waiter went back to the kitchen looking somewhat confused, but eager to please. Now this might seem a bit cruel, but I just had to find out what a plain bastard was.

They gave me a bowl of curd instead, a very nice yoghurt type of affair. As the waiter explained, "Plain bastard not possible, not possible to spice, no bastard possible today."

"Tomorrow?" I ask.

"Maybe tomorrow" he said, "*Maybe* tomorrow."

So this is a book about Neuro-Linguistic Programming (NLP). There are so many NLP books on the shelves that follow the standard formulaic approach of the "Basic Techniques" or "Introduction to—." I believe the last thing the world needs is yet another "Basic Techniques" book, and this definitely isn't one.

After all, NLP just isn't about techniques, but most of you already knew that. This book is at the other end of the spectrum.

The Rainbow Machine

"Close your eyes and tap your heels together three times.
And think to yourself, 'There's no place like home.'"
—The Wizard of Oz

I have spent about ten years working as a nurse. Several years ago I took a temporary agency contract on a children's oncology unit—a member of staff was away on maternity leave. My clinical experience at that time was largely confined to the Accident and Emergency department and Cardiology, so my experience with children was minimal. This temporary placement on children's oncology seemed an ideal place to begin to expand my repertoire as a storyteller and therapist.

At the time an acquaintance from a magical lodge of which I was a member made me a magic storybook—it really was a *magic* storybook because it has those words on the cover. It was huge and very gothic looking, made from thick old-fashioned paper with a cover that looked pretty impressive—all covered with leaves and mirror things. A cunning use of material meant that the surface retained a light dusting of talcum powder, so when I picked it up I could impressively blow off the dust. If you remember the children's TV series, "The Story Teller," this book looked just like that.

Of course the pages of this magnificent book were blank, and the children could choose the story that they'd hear. As the children chose their story, images would begin to appear on the pages in front of them. And if they couldn't see them, well, that was because the wonderful pictures were waiting for them inside their dreams. They only needed to close their eyes to see them, because between us, we'd wake up dreamland with that book. Naturally I would build in lots of metaphor and rhyme relevant to the children's ongoing experiences, and I'd layer-in endless suggestions for healing, comfort and sleep.

I found that when you have a reputation for possessing such a magic book *everyone* wants to hear his or her story being told. A consequence of this was that often my nursing colleagues would accuse me of ignoring the real work while I was slacking off with "those stupid stories."

One morning I was on loan to a neighbouring ward that was short-staffed. A four-year-old girl was crying because she was frightened of going to x-ray. Something about what she had heard about the x-ray must have scared her. Inevitably there were adults surrounding the child who were trying to reassure, coax or force her into "voluntary" co-operation and making the situation far worse. A rule had been made that said she *had* to have an x-ray, and this rule would be enforced even if she had to be sedated or overpowered in order to make it happen. Now, this just wasn't good.

Once I'd managed to pry all these adults away (which is usually the hardest task in such situations), I told her emphatically that *I* didn't want *her* to go to the x-ray room because I didn't want her to know about the secret of the rainbow machine—and then I began to walk away.

"What is the rainbow machine?" She asked.

"I can't tell you; it's a secret," I replied with a hint of a grin.

Now, children are strong *associated* visualisers—they play "Let's pretend," and step into character remarkably well. So full identification with something positive isn't exactly difficult. Look at it this way: NLPers may call it "deep trance identification," but children call it "dressing up" or "play." When I was at school, I was always in the school play—especially at Christmas. Costumes, make-up, face paint and wigs all help maintain and stabilise the trance state into which the child has associated (or chosen to *play*). Kids are simply the best method actors—just give them the right costume, a context in which to operate, a few lines to remember, and they are well on their way.

In a hospital the adults around them do this every day—they put on a white uniform and magically turn into "nurse" or "doctor" or "physio" or whatever. They maintain this all day until they get changed back again and revert once again to "mother," "girlfriend," or whatever. The biggest problem about adults is that they show a remarkable tendency to *forget* that they are playing, and fall into blind obedience to the *rules* of play—which become more important than remembering their original lines. I know about these things, I've bumped into the same people in the supermarket when they are dressed differently and they are *much* less grouchy then when they are in the hospital trance. I'm quite sure that none of them ever intended to be like that—at least, I hope not. I think it must be something about the uniforms—maybe there is too much starch.

"It's a secret, and you are never going to find out what it is, because *I* won't let you. So, *you* have to stay here!" I tell her in a semi-serious, semi-joking voice. In the background, there are two children getting dressed up readying themselves for x-rays. For reasons best known only to themselves they arc covering themselves in tinsel and multi-coloured glitter—I'd got the Christmas box out of the store cupboard earlier. They have managed to spread it everywhere and somehow I just *know* that I am the one who is going to get told off for this later.

"Hurry up," I tell them, "We've got a *rainbow* to catch!"

As soon as these other two are ready, we begin to charge off down the corridor to the rainbow machine room on a lower floor. As we are leaving the room, I cast my eye over to our hero and command, *"Well, come on then!"* She didn't hesitate—she joins us in a flash. So off we go and I grab her a cowboy hat on the way. I have a four-year-old holding one hand, two glitter-covered children leading the way, leaving a sparkling trail, and the three x-ray cards clutched in my other hand.

"Of course," I tell them, "when the rainbow goes inside, it is important to remember where the pot of gold is," as I point and touch, "here," "here," "and here," with all touches made in places relevant to their medical conditions.

"Now who wants to go first?" The radiographer looks at me like I'm nuts. Her look is telling me that it just doesn't work this way; that there are strict rules about these things. Children should be accompanied by the right quota of adults, dressed in the correct clothes and certainly not in groups and almost certainly not having fun in the process.

Later on, I'll be asking these children to paint me a rainbow, complete with the pot of gold. All three paint the same thing—a rainbow *inside a figure* with a pot of gold. The pot of gold is located where the injury or illness was.

Curiously, I've never seen a radiography department any other colour than grey. Even the MRI scanning-tunnel is a drab grey. I suggested psychedelic patterns and dolphins but apparently the management thought that would be "unprofessional." The children's ward is colourful and well-decorated though. It's nice to see a little progress.

Meanwhile I am told off for repeatedly allowing the children to leave glitter trails all over the place and generally leaving a trail of happy disorder everywhere I go.

Self-esteem

*"There is overwhelming evidence that the higher the level
of self-esteem, the more likely one will be to treat others
with respect, kindness, and generosity."*
—Nathaniel Branden

A couple of years ago I was referred a client by a counsellor who had been working with him on an almost weekly basis for more than two years. After all this time (and money!) he finally decided that his own personal version of the Rogerian model of therapy was not helping. The referral letter stated, "Problem: low self-esteem." I agreed to see him.

"I have to learn to like myself," the client informed me when he arrived at my office. "Because only when I like myself can other people like me." Now, that sounded like nonsense to me—the sort of thing someone subjected to too much therapy would say. But I let him ramble on and tell me his story. After an agonising 20 minutes, I interrupted him and took a moment to recapitulate:

"So," I began, "let me check to be sure that I have understood what you have told me. You are miserable. You don't have any friends, and never really had any friends since you left your playgroup and started school. You have a poorly-paid job and everyone there avoids you. You have lunch by yourself every day, and when the others all get together for a drink after work they conveniently fail to invite you. You have never received a Valentine's card that wasn't a joke on you, and your only friend is your mother who still treats you as though you are a child. You have joined singles dating sites on the internet and have failed to get past the first date—if you are lucky enough to get one at all.

So I think I've got some news for you. Your problem *isn't* about low self-esteem or even about liking yourself. Your problem is that *no one likes you, because you are a completely unlikeable person.*

5

Let's face it; no one likes you, not even your counsellor, who was paid to. I *know* he doesn't like you because he sent you to me. I must be honest here—you have sat here in my company for the past twenty minutes driving me mad with your drivel, and I must confess that I don't much like you either. Let's face it, you are utterly unlikable! So I am not at all surprised that you don't like yourself because *you are simply an unlikable guy.*"

A bit of a nasty thing to say, you think? Certainly when I've told this story in seminars, many people are appalled. But you know what happened? He threw his head back and *laughed!* Finally he met someone who took him seriously and would tell him the truth, not some sanitised bullshit that was aimed at sparing his feelings. Finally, he felt *understood.*

Here in front of me was a 40-year-old man with utterly appalling social skills: His trousers were too small yet hitched around his middle, his nails badly cut, his tank-top was a Christmas present from his mother. He cut his own hair, *badly*, and one thing that was unavoidable about this chap was a distinctive odor of something quite unique. Think about it, would *you* want to be his friend? Or would you just feel sorry for him? I had no intention of doing either.

His counsellor had been very sympathetic. I know him; he's a very nice guy with a big heart and enormous patience, but sympathy was the last thing that *this* client needed. What the counsellor failed to see was exactly what was sitting right there in front of him. Maybe he thought the appearance and demeanour of this client was symptomatic of something deeper?

What this client needed most of all was coaching in how to be likeable and get people to like him, including himself. But before we got that far, we had some work to do. First a shower, then a fashionable haircut, then a shopping trip to get him some decent clothes. I telephoned a couple of glitzy female friends whose number one leisure activity is shopping. Their mission was simple, "Make this man *look* and *smell* gorgeous" which is exactly what they did. And of course they fussed over him all afternoon, which was what I was hoping for—he had never had this sort of attention from *one* woman before, much less *two*. On the way home he was sent with orders and the relevant supplies to clear out and clean his apartment. He had bin liners to chuck out all his old clothes, and I told him I'd be checking.

That evening I took him to a wine bar for half an hour. During that time we approached about half a dozen groups of people by asking, "Excuse me, can we borrow just 2 minutes of your time?" I then asked a very simple question: "What are some simple things this guy can do to improve the impression he gives people?" Each time he listened intently. We'd collect the data and move on.

I have done this many times and (surprisingly, to many people I tell about it) no one has ever been offended by our approach or given a rude reply. Most are really keen to help, and find out more about what we are doing. Of course, another aspect of this is that it demonstrates an entirely different side of people to the client.

The following day our session consisted of me teaching him to breathe properly so that he could speak without that horrid nasal tone. We cleared up the remaining social anxieties he still possessed, and I also demonstrated a few useful social skills—like paying attention to *outside* events, and *other* people a bit more.

Toward the end of this he did express a valid concern: "What about when I go back to work? They will all laugh at me for being different." As if they weren't all already doing exactly that! I thought about this for a moment and I knew that he was quite right—they undoubtedly *would* find his attempts at change hilarious. Fellow humans aren't always as supportive as we'd sometimes wish. It may be something in the design somewhere. For whatever reasons, his co-workers might well try to put him back down to the place in the social hierarchy that was supposed to be *his* place, so he needed a strategy to deal with this.

A popular children's game at a playground is "it" (which translates to "tag" on the other side of the Atlantic). The game isn't usually organised but begins with one child running up to another, making some sort of physical contact, and declaring loud enough for everyone to hear, *"You are IT!"* Now, being "it" means everyone runs away from you.

Collectively everyone has decided that having been touched, you are "it." However, an "out" is possible—the child can transfer the "itness" via a touch to another child. Thus he loses the "itness" and the next child is collectively seen as "it." But what if there is no "out"? What if someone remains "it" forever?

Something similar commonly occurs in psychiatric units, where the staff have become accustomed to experiencing the most abnormal behaviours in their patients as being normal for them. Any sudden shift in a patient's behaviour towards the normal can unsettle the status quo quite dramatically, especially when a patient starts gaining confidence and making decisions for himself. The staff unwittingly usually quickly act to put the patient back into the state of "illness." "He's not being himself" is a classic line. If he asserts himself too much, he may provoke a reaction from the staff along the lines of, "Just who does he think he is?"

This kind of dynamic is brilliantly portrayed in Ken Kesey's classic, "*One Flew Over The Cuckoo's Nest*." (26) Especially pertinent is the scene where Nurse Ratched catches out the young patient, Billy, who has successfully managed to lose overnight both his virginity and his crippling stutter—the cure having been brought about by an infraction of the rule structure of the institution. Nurse Ratched engages a most evil strategy to put Billy back into his former identity. She threatens to tell Billy's mother about his behaviour, threatening Billy's identity in the eyes of his mother—Billy is not the child her mother thought she knew. In effect, Billy was once again declared, "it."

I wonder if this kind of need for hierarchy has anything to do with gazelles. Matt Ridley suggests that in order to escape becoming lunch, the average gazelle doesn't need to be able to outrun a cheetah. What he really needs to be able to do is outrun the next nearest *gazelle*. So I wonder if by keeping someone in the status of "patient" it affirms our own position as someone who has a better survival value.

So this client of mine needed an "out" from being tagged with being the "class geek" and the butt of others negative humour. But what he, and the rest of the world, didn't need was to pass the tag of geekyness onto another victim. I jokingly suggested that he wear a T-shirt that had "I AM CHANGING" emblazoned on it. He liked this idea but said, "Wouldn't it be easier to just tell them?'

"Oh, they probably wouldn't listen," I told him, deliberately challenging him to find out how well he could deal with this.

"Well, then I'll just have to *show* them!" he said emphatically.

"*You?*" I said, as though surprised, "How, exactly?'

"I'll just have to learn to be the real *me*, and not the me they want me to be!" he said convincingly, "and if that doesn't work, I'll just tell them I've been hypnotised!"

And with that, I knew his feet were firmly planted on the path.

self belief

Poor Planning

"The road to success is dotted with many tempting parking places."
—Anon.

A few years ago, I tried an experiment. I booked a venue for a one-day weight-loss seminar, one that tends to attract both clients and trainee therapists. I deliberately scheduled it on a day when there would be no refreshments or catering facilities available, and where there were no nearby restaurants or shops. I made this clear in both the advertising and at the point of payment; I advised all attendees that they would need to bring their own lunch and drinks.

At the beginning of the seminar I asked for a show of hands of who had brought food and drink. As I predicted, *only* the people in the room without obvious weight issues raised their hands.

A quick survey and discussion with the participants who had arrived without lunch demonstrated that *every* overweight person in the room had failed to plan to avoid hunger. Their strategy can be summarised as, "We thought we'd worry about it when we got hungry."

Overweight people consistently have a tendency to *react* to hunger, rather than *planning* to avoid it. This repeatedly places them in the position of already being urgently hungry, and needing to eat whatever is immediately available. An analogy is that it works better to put fuel in the car *before* you embark on a long journey, *not afterwards*! This failure to *plan to avoid hunger* is a common strategy.

Stanley Schachter, the brilliant American psychologist, closely examined the eating behaviours of overweight people and animals (42) and noticed some other interesting patterns.

To replicate the hunger urge faced by so many obese people, he studied the behaviour of food-deprived rats. He found that they tended to go only for the food that is most immediately available to them—food that is nearest to them, or doesn't require removal from some obstruction first. In human terms, the rats went for the packets of crisps/chips, pizzas and biscuits rather than leek soup and baked potatoes.

One experiment put people in a context where shelled peanuts were readily available. As predicted, the overweight people ate more peanuts by volume than the people of normal weight. However, when the situation was repeated with *unshelled* peanuts, people who were overweight ate significantly *less* than normal people.

Food-deprived rats also become very finicky about the foods they eat when different food types are again made available to them. They tend to gorge themselves only on food that has a high flavour value; less palatable foods were usually ignored. Schacter found that people tend to follow the same patterns.

In another experiment, he organised a situation where milkshakes were available. As predicted, overweight people tended to consume more milkshake by volume than the people of normal weight.

However, when Schachter organised a repeat scenario, but supplied milkshakes that were adulterated with quinine to give a slightly off-taste, he found that the overweight people actually consumed significantly *less* milkshake by volume than people of normal weight.

These two patterns are common in problem overeaters; they are driven by tastes and flavours, and to food that is immediately available and takes minimal preparation. Food manufacturers know this research well, and produce food-like products ("ready meals") that are high in flavours and take minimal preparation. Supermarket shelves are packed full of pre-packaged products aimed at the person trying to lose weight. However, most of the normally-sized people are in the *other* aisles buying the healthy food that takes time to prepare.

These clients' decision strategies have the same immediacy issue that faces alcoholics, drug addicts, speed freaks and other people with addictive cravings—*they see it and simply **must** have it*—what has been called the "Seafood" diet; they "see food" and eat it. There really isn't any decision strategy in between the stimulus of seeing the food and the response of eating it that would allow them choice; instead it is replaced with a set of simple conditioned responses. Meanwhile, their *motivation* strategy consists of a direct visual stimulus to kinaesthetic response, and the images are still pictures, rather than movies. That suggested to me that changing their images into movies that go through time might be very useful.

At weight-loss seminars I tell the participants to go out to a supermarket and return with a food that drives their strongest craving. Almost invariably this will be some pre-packaged, high flavour, high fat junk food, such as crisps, biscuits, chocolate cake and the like.

Then I tell participants to look at their chosen food and encourage them to get the craving up to a full maximum.

Then I ask them to close their eyes and focus on the image they have of the cake, or whatever it is, and imagine taking a bite, *just one at first*, and then to imagine chewing and tasting it thoroughly as well. . . *and then another*, . . . and *another*. I have them imagine eating the entire thing in this way until they have finished. In order to do this, they have to create a *movie* of the sequence of bites. Then I have them eat another one in the same way, one bite at a time, *chewing and tasting each bite thoroughly*. I then ask how they feel. Almost always they respond that they no longer want the cake, or that they feel sick, full, guilty, or whatever it is they usually feel *after* they've gorged themselves.

Then I ask them to run their movie even further ahead in time to include being on the scales the next day, feeling guilty about having eaten the cake and so on. With a number of repetitions, this becomes a new pattern. Instead of eating the entire cake before feeling the regret, remorse, guilt, or whatever it is, they can learn to feel these feelings *before* they eat the cake. This is a very effective way of reducing impulsive behaviours.

And I get to go home after these seminars laden with all the goodies left behind! *Great!*

A Case of Dying

*"It's only when we truly know and understand that we have
a limited time on earth—and that we have no way of knowing
when our time is up, we will then begin to live each day
to the fullest, as if it was the only one we had."*
—Elizabeth Kubler-Ross

An oncology patient, an 8-year-old child, is close to death. Although he isn't directly one of my patients, I have good rapport with him. It is clear that he isn't going to make it, despite the best efforts of everybody involved. Surrounding him are adults, all trying to deal with this awful situation.

Quite understandably, these adults are not coping particularly well, and from what I can see, this child is quite confused by what is going on. A very difficult dynamic occurs between visitors and relatives and a dying adult. Both tend to struggle to maintain a semblance of normality and not allow their emotions to show through too much. In effect, people put on a mask of safety. When the dying person is a child, and no one has explicitly told the child what is happening, much confusion can occur as the child tries to make sense of what's going on.

With this particular little guy, the confusion is apparent. He is sullen and pale. So, I loiter in the background, pacing the room. I know I've paced enough when he calls me.

"Andy?" his small voice asks, "Am I going to die?" It's the very question that everyone has been doing their very best to avoid confronting. Some things just hurt too much. There is a deathly silence apart from a sudden muffled sobbing somewhere in the background.

"Yes." I reply, "Yes you are." I say it calmly, but inside I am terrified of the other adults' reaction. A dying child I can mostly handle—but a room full of emotional adults might just prove to be difficult, and this may not go the way I am intending. It is not often that I take this sort of risk.

"Oh," he said, "I *thought* so," and he relaxed and smiled. "I thought maybe I'd done something wrong." He looked more alive now, rather than sullen and subdued as he was before. Now he understood why everyone was acting so strangely around him. Death had never been raised as an issue.

"It's OK, Mum," he said to reassure her, before going on to tell her about his grandmother who was waiting for him, the angels, Jesus and all sorts of other things. He was now able to talk about these things because the *adults* around him were now permitted to talk about them. He died peacefully later that week, knowing that he was loved, and knowing that he hadn't done anything wrong.

Satan

*"We may not pay Satan reverence, for that would be indiscreet, but
we can at least respect his talent"*   —Mark Twain

With hindsight, maybe dressing up as Satan *was* a step too far,
but sometimes I just cannot resist. When a consultant psychiatrist
called me up to book an appointment to "confront her Catholic guilt"
then something inside my head just started shouting, *"Go on!! She's
a psychiatrist! Do it!! Do the session dressed as Satan!!"*

Living less than a mile from the best fancy dress hire shop in
town meant the logistics for this were easy. A week passed to the
appointment.

So with curtains closed, a large pentagram drawn in heavy chalk
on the office carpet, five black candles and heavy myrrh incense
burning at each point of the pentagram, the scene was perfectly set.
The doorbell rang, and I opened the door.

"Andy?" She asked, confused, evidently thinking that she must
have made a mistake. It was 9:00 AM and Wednesday. Right time.
Right place.

"Yes," I said with minimal facial expression and a flat intonation.

"Andy *Austin?*" She asked, cautiously, seeking clarification.

"Yes," I said, not smiling nor moving. She didn't say anything
else. She just raised her eyebrows expectantly, whilst looking to me
for some kind of direction. Needless to say, I didn't give it.

We stood there for about 20 seconds staring at each other. Me
dressed as Satan, and her looking like a confused and frightened rabbit about to get run over by something she would never get time to
understand.

"Umm, . . ." she said, breaking the silence, probably hoping I
would help her out. Needless to say I wouldn't. The pungent smoke
from the incense kept wafting over us through the doorway.

"Can I come in?" she ventured nervously.

"Oh yes!" I said, *"Yes you may."* And I reached out and led her by the hand across the pentagram into my darkened and candle-lit office. . . .

Rather than ask about them, I had totally aroused *all* her responses to religion—in spades. She got the point that the stunt was aimed at her dropping her consultant psychotherapist role, and she sat down and began by saying:

"I think I know what my problem *really* is. My problem is that I am locked into a dysfunctional co-dependency where my inner child isn't being nurtured appropriately."

Now these are the kind of words spoken only by someone who has read far too many self-help books, or received way too much therapy or psychiatric training.

I fixed her with a demonic stare and said, "In that case I know exactly what you need. . . . When there is a problem with an inner child, the only thing you need is, (I raised my eyebrows, and paused, to get her full attention) . . . you need a *fucking* abortion!"

The use of the vernacular was quite intentional, and the abreaction that my obnoxious suggestion elicited was quite spectacular. I sat there patiently whilst this psychiatrist savagely ripped into my attitude, my conduct, my professionalism, my language, and so forth.

I waited until she finished and took a breath. "Is there anything else you would like to shout at the devil?" I asked her quietly. She sat there for a moment looking shocked. Then her mouth moved up and down as she struggled to work out quite what she wanted to say. I pointed my trident at her and said with a hint of a smile, "Mmmmm? Well?"

She broke into a smile and said, "I don't think I like you."

"I know," I told her, "Few people do. Want to sell me your soul?"

From that point the session continued fairly routinely, as we "unpacked" her reactions to what I had said, and explored her beliefs and values. At that time, my fee was only around forty pounds per session. At the end of the session she handed me a cheque for £250 and thanked me for what I had done.

People often ask me how I have the nerve to carry out such stunts. Well, I blame the naivete of youth—it rarely even occurs to me to do them anymore, and I must say, I definitely suffer much less anxiety as a result!

Word Salad Dave

To say he was happy may not be appropriate. However, people who met him thought that Word Salad Dave *appeared* to be happy. With an endless stream of bizarre and incomprehensible babble, Dave's speech sounded happy enough, and his bodily mannerisms and occasional chuckle made him out to be a happy and confused fool.

Dave had strange relationships with all sorts of animals, including the fish, which were accidentally killed off twice by the appearance of large quantities of potato chips in the tank—"fish and chips." Dave sometimes believed that the departmental budgies were plotting something. One day their cage inexplicably vanished from the living room and was located later that day suspended about 30 feet up a fir tree deep into the institution's extensive grounds.

The mystery of how this happened was solved the following day when the budgies' guardian, a burly schizophrenic called Jenny, spotted Dave, wearing a tea towel as a bandana, and the budgies leaving the building with a dozen nylon stockings knotted together, a tin of beans and a roll of masking tape. The budgies were safely returned to the lounge and a round-the-clock budgie guard was initiated by concerned residents, who protected them from Dave with a rolled-up newspaper and a cricket ball.

Naturally, the staff psychiatrist started him on some heavy duty anti-psychotic drugs; the word salad stopped, and the budgies went unmolested.

The laughter stopped too, and Dave spent much of his time in a stupor in the day room. The budgie guard was disbanded and a safe departmental monotony was restored.

"The Child"

Boy: "Mummy! Look what a big fat worm I have got!"
Mother: "You are filthy—away and clean yourself immediately!"
—R.D. Laing, (32, p.102)

When I am asked to work with a child, I will often go to the family home for a while to gather information. Seeing someone's living environment can yield a lot of very useful information that I otherwise wouldn't get. One day I found myself observing the interaction between a mother and her "defiant" and "severely hyperactive" five-year-old son. The parents had informed me that this child—who not *once* was referred to by name, but rather as "the child"—was "utterly uncooperative" and would be "impossible to control" owing to his Attention Deficit Disorder and his apparent unwillingness to listen to his parents.

The child is rolling around on the ground in the garden. I think he is pretending to be a caterpillar.

In a stern voice, the mother addresses the child: "I don't think my washing machine is going to get those clothes clean!" (I think what she means is that she would like the child to stop rolling around in the dirt.)

The child ignores his mother and carries on rolling around as only a happy little caterpillar might do.

Mother (with increased emphasis): "I guess you expect me to provide your clothes for free?!"

The child continues to ignore his mother. After all, he hasn't the slightest idea what she is talking about!

Mother (turns to me): "You see?!! He never listens to a word I say!"

I am a bit skeptical about "Attention Deficit Disorder" as a valid diagnosis in this case; what seemed to be the problem here was the ambiguity and the indirectness of the parents' communications to their child. The mother's initial response to her child's behaviour was to refer to her washing machine, and I don't know many five-year-olds who have the slightest interest in washing machines. It is most unlikely that any five-year-old will be able to translate that statement into one that asks him to get up out of the dirt. In fact, it is quite possible that the child will not even think of the message as being intended for him at all, since it is so far removed from the experience of any 5-year-old.

At this point the child appears to turn into a tractor and starts shunting clods of earth around the flowerbeds. His father enters the scene. He and his wife exchange knowing looks. Mother sighs in resignation, and father turns a bit red with anger and whines:

"You never listen to a word your mother says!" followed by,

"We only planted those flowers last week!'

The child glances over at his father before uprooting a daffodil, giving father a look that suggested something along the lines of, "So fucking what?" and begins to uproot all the flowers in the vicinity.

It was at this point in the proceedings that the mother went crying to the cupboard to fetch the Ritalin (she was worried about her fuchsias) as the father reminded the child, "You *never* listen to a word your mother says!"

To which the child raised his head briefly and gave a look that said, "OK, Dad, if you say so."

An interesting ambiguity reflected the family dynamic of the supposed attention deficit disorder when the mother said, "Thank God the doctor gave *us* Ritalin!" To which I was naturally tempted to ask just how much *she* was taking.

In order to save the beloved fuchsias, I asked the child, by name, what would be a useful thing for a tractor to do, and then suggested that we replant the flowers. Joining him down there in the dirt, we began to replant the uprooted flowers—he dug, I planted. All the while, the parents lamented about how dirty I would get because of "the child."

His name was Danny.

Patching Holes

*Miracle: "Specifically: An event or effect contrary
to the established constitution and course of things, or a deviation
from the known laws of nature; a supernatural event, or one
transcending the ordinary laws by which the universe is governed."*
—Webster's Dictionary.

I cannot help but wonder how different world history would be if Jesus had gone around *boasting* of his miracles. I can picture it now, Jesus by the river with his friends, regaling them with the Lazarus story for the umpteenth time, or showing off how a mere crucifixion was no match for *His* superior talents. The follow-up to that whole set of events might have been very different indeed. There is a certain wisdom in all holy books about keeping quiet about miracles, that really should be paid attention to.

For many in the healing professions, performing the apparently miraculous is a common affair. It is, after all, what one is paid to do. As a staff nurse in neurosurgery I had a patient with a rare condition known as a syrinx. Essentially a syrinx is a fluid-filled cavity within the spinal cord that enlarges over time and can result in devastation to that part of the spinal cord and nerve roots. Imagine a bicycle inner tube bulging through a split in an old worn tire.

A 40-year-old man had undergone various neurological investigations, including a spinal tap that had unfortunately resulted in a syrinx. Repeated attempts at treating this condition had failed, and his situation was looking grim.

When I came across this gentleman he was ashen in colour, agitated and very angry. I wasn't sure of his understanding of what he was facing or what he was experiencing, but it did not take great sensitivity to realise that it wasn't positive.

"How you doing?" I ask him.

"Fuck off!" he growls angrily.

"No," I replied, evenly, "I'm not fucking off. What's up?" I ask innocently.

"*What's up*? I'm going to be fucking paralysed, *that* is *what's up*," he sneered.

"And how do you know that?" Now I am aware of how terribly annoying this last question can be. NLP practitioners who have recently learned the meta-model tend to ask this much too often, and not always with any thought to why they are asking it. However, on this occasion I knew exactly where I was going.

This is the sort of situation in which a colleague of mine looks around on the walls, and says, "Let me see your fortune-telling license," to draw attention to the fact that the person is making a prediction about the future without being suitably trained and qualified.

"What?!" My patient growled, clearly annoyed at both my continuing presence and the nature of the question. As a health care professional involved in his care, I really should know more than I appeared to know.

I asked again, "How do you know that you are going to be *fucking paralysed*"? His eyes go up and to the left, then up and to the right. Then back up to the left again.

"There are only so many times that you can put a patch over a punctured inner tube. When a patch doesn't work, you can only put so many patches over the top before you ruin the fucking thing. *That* is how I know!" It was obvious that he had a very clear representation of this.

"I think you are wrong on that," I say quietly. "An inner tube is not a living thing. It is black, dirty, and dead. Have you ever actually seen a living spinal cord?" I asked, as I gestured up to his right. His manner changed dramatically. Now he was attentive and curious, instead of angry. I really didn't think it was going to be this easy.

I sketch it with my hands. "A spinal membrane is a living matrix. It lives. It is a good healthy colour, even when damaged; under a microscope the cells look beautiful. That is why I think you have the wrong picture." I move my hands out, as though enlarging the picture.

"Shit!" he says, a better colour coming into his face. "I had never thought about it that way."

"That's right," I say, "you *didn't*" and quietly walk away.

Before my long shift was over, this man was eating again and laughing and joking with the staff. Eight hours later his syrinx was found to have mysteriously vanished. Eight hours was all it took! It is a testament to the healing ability that is latent in every living organism. I cannot really claim any particular credit for this minor miracle; after all, I was simply applying something I had been taught. (1, ch. 20) But at the time I was excited. This was amazing, and I just *had* to share it with the other staff.

A word of advice—don't ever do this with nurses; they simply do not understand, and always love an opportunity to ridicule the strange man. Teach what is possible, but don't claim credit for *making* it possible; that is bad medicine. Since this lesson, I have also learned that the best NLP masters rarely ever mention NLP when they are working out in the world. They just *do* it.

Bedwetting

"Obviously one must hold oneself responsible for the evil impulses of one's dreams. In what other way can one deal with them? Unless the content of the dream rightly understood is inspired by alien spirits, it is part of my own being." —Sigmund Freud

I am often consulted by people experiencing problems that typically would be considered too embarrassing to talk about publicly, or even to a doctor or therapist—sexual dysfunctions, anxieties such as impotence and premature ejaculation, odd compulsions and attractions, and the troublesome secret thoughts usually kept very private from anyone else. Unsurprisingly, most of these consultations are initiated via email.

Adult bedwetting is one such hidden problem, one that is rarely discussed in any public forum. Since bedwetting (enuresis) is associated with small children, adult bedwetting is often met with derision, sarcasm and ridicule. The personal consequences are kept private, so it remains a subject about which the majority of people, including some therapists, remain ignorant. And since it is a hidden topic, the chances of getting help to change it are extremely slim.

The consequences of adult bedwetting can be huge. Intimate relationships may be avoided (often to the mystification of friends and family), there may be a sense of inadequacy and shame, and low self-esteem is common. The affected person may avoid holidays and any other overnight stays away from home.

Bedwetting is not caused by a particular psychological problem. In fact, whilst the bedwetting itself can certainly *result* in particular problems, adult bedwetters are no more screwed up than any other portion of the population. Adults have been wetting beds for as long as there have been adults and beds.

Searching for a "deep-rooted" psychological problem is undoubtedly unnecessary, and is potentially counterproductive. From my experience of listening to client's stories, far too many have learned to have *new* problems whilst in therapy. Despite the frustration of previous failures, the adult bedwetter is not a useless victim of a hopeless condition who must simply learn to live with their problem.

Freud wrote that dreams were the "royal road to the unconscious." I'm not sure about royalty, but certainly dreams can be interesting when it comes to bedwetting. I can still remember the dreams I had as a young child that always resulted in a wet bed. I was always in the garden of "Mary, Mary Quite Contrary." I didn't know who Mary was, or why she was quite contrary, but I did know the secret of how her garden grew—I kept peeing into her watering can.

My young brain and unconscious mind was managing to protect my need for sleep and also respond to my physical need to urinate. So it created a story whereby urinating while sleeping was legitimized.

I used to wake up shivering, usually some time afterwards when the wetness had lost its warmth, and shout for my parents that the bed was wet. I always knew that I was the one who wet the bed, but I could never actually say it. I maintained a certain distance from the problem by saying, "The bed is wet," rather than, "I wet the bed."

This all changed when my father asked me one day, "Well, who wet it?" To maintain my dissociation I lied and I said, "I don't know." He gently coaxed me that this wasn't actually true, and that in fact I did know. After some persuasion I admitted that I *did* know, and that it *was* actually me. I remember feeling a significant level of shame that day, and never again did I wet the bed.

Taking ownership of a problem can be a painful moment for many adults too, even though it is often an essential first step toward making a change. The most common way of not taking ownership is to utilise the "illusion of ownership" technique illustrated by the following justifications, (or "reasons," "excuses," or however you might like to think of them):

"I have a condition." (The condition causes the problem.)

"It's my nerves." (The nerves are responsible.)

"It's a genetic disorder." (The genes are responsible.)

"It is because of my childhood" (My childhood is responsible).

"It is just the way I am made." (The way I am made is responsible.)

"It's because of stress." (Stress is responsible.)

"I've always been this way." (The past is responsible.)

Try the following exercise to test for the difference in how each statement feels to you. Say the following either out loud or inside your mind and compare your feelings:

1. "The bed gets wet." (Psychologically easy to accept.)

2. "I wet the bed." (Psychologically difficult to accept.)

1. "Bedwetting is a problem I experience." (Psychologically easy to accept.)

2. "I am the one who creates my experience." (Psychologically difficult to accept.)

Taking psychological ownership of a problem isn't easy, but if you are to take control of it, it is a vital step towards creating personal change.

After my painful confession and taking ownership of the behaviour, I noticed a significant change in my dreams. Now my unconscious mind had another thing to protect me from. In addition to allowing me to continue sleeping, it needed to respond to my need to urinate in a way that avoided another day of shame.

I forgot about Contrary Mary, whom I understand now was actually a reference to Mary Queen of Scots, and instead of a royal watering can, I hunted for a variety of other legitimate places to pee. I still dreamed of needing to urinate, but for some reason I could never reach the place to pee into. The toilet was too far away, it was too high, there were monsters in the way, there was a long queue, the toilet was too small, I didn't have the right entry ticket, or I simply couldn't find it. Despite my urgent need to pee, I would continue sleeping, dreaming of not being able to find or reach the toilet. Sometimes the signal would eventually register in the right part of my brain, and I'd wake up and use the bathroom. Not once have I ever dreamed that I had woken up and used a dream bathroom by mistake—that would have risked shame, of course.

A colleague once told me about the dream he had that was the trigger for his bedwetting. As a child, he learned the words of the nursery rhyme of "Oranges and Lemons," also known as the "London Bells," which ends with that lovable line, "Here comes a candle to light you to bed, here comes a chopper to chop off your head."

The words and verses in this rhyme tend to vary according to geographical region, and when John was seven, his family moved and he was relocated to a different school. On his first day there the teacher organised a children's game oriented around the rhyme, which had an extra verse.

Since he was unfamiliar with the words, another child joked that that meant that John would have to have his head "cut off" in accordance with the game. For poor John, already worried and disoriented by his first day at the new school—well, this was almost too much for the poor guy. Later, on the playground, another anxious child confided in John that he knew that bad people hid choppers in the rafters of old houses which would sometimes come down and chop the sleeping person's head off in the night.

By the time he got home that day, poor John was a nervous wreck. Although he had had a dry bed since the age of four, he became a fervent bedwetter for several years, complete with disturbing nightmares. John quickly settled into the new school and made new friends, but the nocturnal anxiety continued.

Since the bedwetting and nightmares started at exactly the time that he changed house and school, it was put down to an understandable stress response resulting from the move. His parents asked the obvious questions: was he being bullied? Did he have a problem with his teacher? Was there some other obvious external cause?

What they couldn't have known though, was the power of childhood imagination and subjective realities. John *knew* there were choppers in the rafters just waiting to chop off his head because he did not know the right words to a stupid nursery rhyme. Strangely, many children learn not to discuss such fears with adults. I guess they know that adults don't really understand such things. Reexamining these unconscious beliefs from the perspective and knowledge of an adult released him from his childhood prison.

Several years ago I worked with a young man who had had a problem with bedwetting since childhood. The pattern hadn't really altered despite his age, and approximately three or four times a week, he would wake up and the bed would be wet. The pattern seemed entirely random except for the fact that as a child he *never* wet the bed when he was staying anywhere other than his family home.

Despite being understandably anxious about the potential for disaster, school trips didn't present a problem, nor did staying at friends' houses. Despite this conscious knowledge, his anxiety about staying elsewhere persisted and his social life and social development suffered as a result. He presented to me as a shy 20-something who was not achieving his full potential, still living at home with his parents.

Whilst I was taking a complete history, several interesting details emerged. Some people wet the bed because they sleep so soundly they have difficulty waking up. But this guy didn't sleep very well, so that wasn't the problem.

His mother said something interesting to me, "When he was small, he was always quite an overactive child, and he would often get up in the night and wander 'round the house." It was after this nocturnal wandering that the bedwetting behaviour emerged as a problem.

Now it occurred to me that every parent wants to be able to sleep soundly at night, knowing that his or her child is tucked up in bed—not wandering around the house. So, if a child does wander, the likely injunction from the parent is to "Stay in bed." So I couldn't help but wonder if despite the signals of needing to use the bathroom, his unconscious mind was still obeying an old parental command to "Stay in bed—no matter what!"

Using light hypnosis, I simply gave him the suggestion that whilst staying in bed at all costs had been important when he was a child, now that he was a grown man he was indeed able to become aware, unconsciously at first, that he could make certain decisions for himself, and he could become conscious of the bodily and physical requirements to which he needed to pay more attention. In short, his unconscious mind needed permission not to wake up, but to get out of bed and use the bathroom. Unconscious minds work in mysterious ways; the problem disappeared, quite literally, overnight. Since then, I have had a number of other clients who simply needed permission to disobey an old parental injunction of this kind.

There is another method that is very successful in treating bedwetting called "paradoxical intention," that turns all logic on its head. Developed by psychiatrist and holocaust survivor Viktor Frankl (21) paradoxical intention has an astonishing success rate. The essence of the technique is that the person makes a mental shift from trying to *not* have the problem, to actively engaging in *doing* the problem.

So for example, the panic attack sufferer deliberately practices having panic attacks, the nail biter deliberately bites their nails, the insomniac is encouraged to lie still and try and stay awake as long as possible, and so on. When someone does this, the unconscious impulses that drive the behaviour begin to move into consciousness—and thus potentially come under conscious control. As a therapist I have found this especially helpful with problems such as blushing and anxiety.

What this means for the adult bedwetter is that rather than trying to *eliminate* the problem, they consciously *produce* the problem. As unpleasant as it might sound, getting into bed with a full bladder and deliberately urinating in the bed is the first step.

Now, just deliberately wetting the bed isn't enough. You must not change the sheets until morning. What you have ahead of you is the uncomfortable experience of deliberately spending the night in a wet bed.

As you can imagine, sleep is unlikely to be very easy. Despite lack of sleep, you must carry on your activities the next day, so the experiment must be integrated into your normal daily routine—not sectioned off as a special event that is unconnected.

Understandably, enuretic clients are very reluctant to try this method, and most therapists are equally reluctant to suggest it. I tell clients to do this every night for a month, even if the problem disappears during the first week. I find their reluctance quite understandable—despite the fact that many of them are wetting the bed every day of the month already anyway!

When I propose this task, I always listen very carefully to the objections they raise about doing it. Often very useful information arises regarding the unconscious nature of the problem. Take a moment to imagine that you are a bedwetter, and write down *all* your own objections to doing this. . . .

The client is instructed to carefully attend to *all* their thoughts, objections, excuses, and so forth and write them down. I describe the effect to my students as, "Unconscious material comes gushing out when you engage clients in paradoxical intention, so be sure to catch it all."

Classic objections are, "That is disgusting!" "I couldn't possibly do that!" "That is far too much to expect of me!" "How can you possibly expect me to do that?" and so forth. On examination of the beliefs that underlie these statements and protestations we can find some interesting material. When I challenged his "That is disgusting!" statement, one client said, "Because if I do it deliberately, it means that I am some kind of weirdo or pervert or something." As we explored this belief, the client recalled a period in his hormonally-charged teenage years where he experienced urination as a sexually arousing act. Disturbed by these experiences, he tried to shut out thoughts of urination and sexual arousal, but they still bothered him at an unrecognised level.

Bridging the gap between the unconscious nocturnal activity with paradoxical intention is a very effective technique that is simple, cheap, and easily applied. However it does require a degree of gumption to be able to actually do it, both because it is very unpleasant, and because it flies in the face of everything the adult bedwetter has been trying to do all those years.

The Long Stand

"Wait there!"—Command given to a psychiatric patient on arrival in the secure seclusion room.

As a teenager, I worked in a large department store. The wages and hours were good, the management fair and efficient, and the staff loyal. This lent itself to a certain fun atmosphere and practical jokes were common. Often lockers would be booby-trapped with flour bombs, or packed tightly with foam packing beads awaiting the unsuspecting victim to open the door.

Meanwhile there is a man standing in the warehouse. . . . It's an old joke but it still endures. Every new guy was sent out to the store next door for the classic left-handed screwdriver, tin of elbow grease, or out to the warehouse to find that tin of tartan paint. But the most common one was, "Go to the warehouse and ask for a long stand." Everyone knew this one, and when Dave the warehouse supervisor was faced with a new guy full of acne and nervousness, he knew the drill. "Yes, just wait there. . . ." he'd say, and walk off.

Nervous people tend to do as they are told *even if they suspect it is false,* and I swear that guy is still standing there, still waiting, waiting, waiting. . . .

Years later I once sent a request to the hospital portering department to collect a box of fallopian tubes from the gynaecology department. Almost inevitably I was taken aside and "spoken to." Apparently with manpower and time resources being so scarce, hoax requests of this type were not appreciated. When I sent a request to maintenance to collect the "broken menstrual cycle" from the physiotherapy department, the chief porter positively blew a gasket.

29

Sarah, Dominatrix

Sarah, a friend of mine from my student nurse days, soon learned that the life of a nurse is seldom quite as glamorous as some people think it is. I should know—I worked as a hospital nurse for 10 years; it can be a thankless job at the best of times. For two of those years I worked in neurosurgery and most of my day was spent making beds and clearing up shit, vomit, sputum and God knows what else. Juices just seem to get everywhere in neurosurgery. Although badly paid, this is valuable and essential work.

When I'd meet people socially, the inevitable question would come, "So Andrew, what is it that you do?" When I'd reply, "I work in neurosurgery" people would either look at me in utter disbelief (I guess I don't look the type) or gaze at me in total awe, as though I was some kind of reverent being. But realistically, the majority of my work there was a long way from being glamorous or even remotely heroic.

Having worked as a nurse for more than enough years, Sarah decided it was time to move on. Not really knowing what else to do for money, Upper-Middle-Class Sarah—with a facial expression that said that butter wouldn't melt in her mouth—decided to become a dominatrix. She converted her garage into a dungeon, invested in some leather gear, placed a small advert in the local paper and started charging £200 per 30-minute spanking session. She didn't consider her line of work to be prostitution, since she never made any skin-to-skin contact with any of her clients.

"It is weird," she told me, "I have spent years safeguarding people's dignity and respect, and have been paid appallingly. Now I beat, abuse, and humiliate people and I'm paid a fortune!"

"I used to spend time with my hands up people's backsides and washing people's genitals on the wards," she said, "but at least in this job I can be honest—I loathe these pathetic perverts and I tell them so. Yet they love me for it, and keep coming back for more."

Critical Self-talk

Typical patterns of spoken internal criticism.

"I am" patterns.

"I am such a loser."

"I am an idiot."

"I am useless."

And so on.

"You are" patterns, where the self is the target.

"You are such a loser."

"You are an idiot."

"You are useless."

And so on.

"I hate" patterns set up a negative relationship between the person and their "self"; one part of themselves feels hate, the other feels hated.

"I hate myself."

"I hate my problem."

"I hate the way I behave."

And so on.

Negative future programming: self-hypnosis or auto-suggestion patterns.

"I won't ever change."

"I'll feel this way forever."

"This problem will never go away."

And so on.

Now think about it. You wouldn't talk to anyone *else* that way, would you? Yet somehow most people think it is OK to talk to *themselves* that way. If *you* do this, then you really should be ashamed of yourself, and apologise to yourself immediately. Sincerely.

Instead, be *nice* to yourself for a change. You wouldn't bully a child to change his or her behaviour and then expect him or her to be

31

happy with the change. And I hope you don't shout at someone else repeatedly to help build their confidence—so be nice and stop all your negative self-talk.

There are several ways I like to manouvre clients into realizing how their internal dialogue affects them, and also how to get control over it. One method is to get the client to verbalise the patterns out loud, deliberately and consciously to *me* as though I am the object of their negativity. I'm told that Fritz Perls, (35) founder of Gestalt Therapy, often did this, telling the client, "Say it to me; I can fight back."

There are two fairly typical responses to this. Firstly, since the client has rarely ever said these things deliberately and out loud before, it is unfamiliar, and they often report that it feels silly. This is good. Before, the words they used internally felt natural and normal to say. Now, they *feel* different; they feel silly.

Secondly, clients often express that it feels wrong to be saying such things. Again this is good. In my map of the world, it *is* wrong to say such things, since rarely does any good come from it. So I encourage the client to continue saying more and more of the patterns, increasingly expressing mock horror that they could say such things to me.

Me: "So you think you have the right to judge me, do you?"

Client (protesting): "But I was just saying what you asked me to say."

Me: "And so you thought that gives you the right to tell me that I was worthless, is that what you think? Mmmm?"

And then I spring my trap. I increasingly reduce my mock level of offence and rapidly escalate my responses into what is *genuine* offense. At first the client laughs it off, experiencing my acting for what it is. But as my state worsens, the client is unable to shake it off. The atmosphere becomes unpleasant and tense, and I start demanding answers and explanations. It can then go something like this:

Client: "Look, I didn't mean to upset you or anything."

Me: "Yeah, right. So *you* get the privilege to measure how successful I get to be in life, and I have to listen to such crap, right?"

I continue this until I reach a plateau in the interaction and then, mid-sentence and in a flash, I suddenly switch state to a very pleasant and smiley one and offer the client a cup of tea. This enables me to leave the room for a few minutes whilst the client's confused brain turns somersaults trying to figure out what the hell just happened.

By taking on the role of the recipient of the negative verbal suggestions—and fighting back—it forces the client to dramatically change their position, and this is remarkably effective. I am also modeling for the client how they can vigorously refute what the self-talk says.

However, it is important to know that this can be rather stressful on the client, so you need to be very attentive to their response. Students who observe me doing this tend to squirm uncomfortably, and later express surprise that I actually do such things. "Isn't there a nicer way to get the same result?" is often the theme of their questions.

There are other ways, of course—there *always* are; the trick is getting the client to actually do them. Fritz Perls—famous for his utilization of furniture—used two chairs to separate the two positions the client adopts with their internal dialogue. Chair one might be for the criticizer; chair two for the criticisee. When the client sits in one of the two chairs they take on the part represented by that position, and switch periodically to the other chair to respond.

This way the client gets to experience consciously what has been occurring spontaneously at a relatively unconscious level, and clearly separate the two aspects of self-criticism. This makes the situation much clearer, and often the client is able to work through the issues involved, although some clients (and some therapists) may well find the whole process somewhat bizarre.

When someone thinks, "I hate myself" I like to find out if the issue is with the "I" doing the hating, or if it is with the self being hated—or some mixture of the two. Either way, hating something is rarely helpful in promoting change.

A very effective method that spilled out of NLP is to change the submodalities of the critical voice. I prefer to worsen the submodalities first, before restoring them to their normal level. For example, making a critical voice louder will usually intensify the negative feelings; then they can reduce the volume back to its normal level, and that becomes a reference experience for reducing the intensity further—something that was invariably missing form their previous ongoing experience.

Adjusting speed—making a critical voice faster and faster, then slower and slower can also be very effective as a precursor to change. People can usually do this quite readily, and will often say that the voice now sounds silly. This is a good start, because the client has just demonstrated to themselves their ability to change something consciously.

Once the simple submodality changes enable the client to realise that they can change the internal critical voice, changing the accent can have a profound impact. Regional accents can be useful too. Most cultures have accents that other people tend to find humorous, irritating, or unusual in some way. Personally, I changed mine to that of my favorite comedian, complete with canned audience laughter. With a bit of repetition the changes generalize, which is when I begin to challenge the presumptions of the *content* of the internal dialogue.

"So how you do you know that you are not actually useless? I mean, maybe you are?" This is the kind of question I like to joke with to the client—gently provoking the negative responses whilst eliciting humour. Humour is always a useful state that provides great leverage in any persistent problem, no matter what you think might be useful to do next.

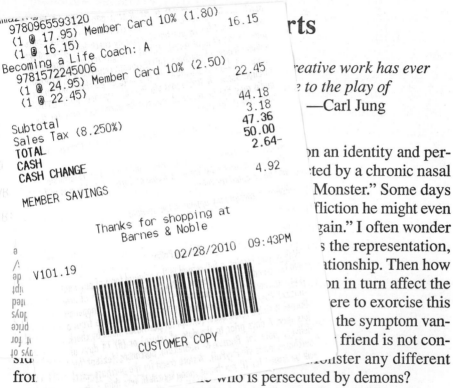

...rts

...reative work has ever
... to the play of
—Carl Jung

...on an identity and per-...ted by a chronic nasal ... Monster." Some days ...fliction he might even ...gain." I often wonder ...s the representation, ...ationship. Then how ...on in turn affect the ...ere to exorcise this ... the symptom van-... friend is not con-...nster any different fror... ...who is persecuted by demons?

... years ago in the UK a cancer clinic engaged in an interesting series of experiments in visualisation with cancer patients. The patients were to visualise their disease and imagine it changing, either by visualising it shrinking, or being eaten up by the appropriate blood cells. A patient might even visualize an army of little helpers dismantling the tumour. Essentially what is being asked and expected of the client is that they can find a way of gaining access to a physiological change response via visualisation. After many years the evidence for this still remains controversial, but there is a lot of anecdotal evidence that at least for *some* people such a technique can be of benefit.

I once attended a group session held by an acquaintance of mine, and I could quickly see a serious flaw in her method. Using a very effective relaxation technique, the patients were then directed in how to visualise their disease, ("See it as a dark, soft mass") and then amongst other suggestions, to see white blood cells attacking and reducing the dark soft mass. Her instruction revealed how *she* visualises a malignant disease, but it doesn't necessarily match what her clients unconsciously experience.

Connirae Andreas' technique for enhanced healing (1, ch. 20) uses a visualization that is elicited from the individual concerned, not dictated and imposed arbitrarily from outside by the therapist. It is also different in that it utilises the *client's* experience of something that has *already healed*, so that presupposes that the visualization will have the desired effect.

I'm always interested in the metaphors people use to describe their afflictions. For example, it is not uncommon for people to say things like, "My legs turned to jelly," or "I have a lump in my throat." In each of these instances we know that their legs aren't really made of jelly, and that there usually isn't really a lump in their throat, despite a very convincing sensation that suggests otherwise. But if we were to pursue the representation out of the kinaesthetic modality and add in the visual, we usually find that we have much more to work with.

For example, here's a simple extract from a demonstration with one of my clients who is describing the negative feelings that occur in a certain context:

Client: "I get this lump in my throat."

Good Looking Therapist: "And . . . it is there, now . . ." (Spoken as a command, with downward inflection, but with raised eyebrows, requesting a response.)

I want to clarify a few points here. "It is *there, now* . . ." is a command to gain immediate access to the symptom. If the client answers, "Yes," well and good. If she answers, "No it isn't" I would simply have responded with an "as if" frame, "So tell me, if it *were* to *be there now,* how would it feel?"

GLT: "Now, if that lump were to have a shape, what sort of shape would it have?" I lead her to add to the representation by asking a question that doesn't specify modality. She can either *see* a shape, or *feel* a shape; it doesn't really matter. Either one will fill out the representation.

C: "Round, but not smooth—like a rock."

When she says, "It is like a rock," I can deduce with reasonable certainty that it is heavy, it is hard, and that it is more likely to be gray or black than bright pink or orange. These aspects of her experience are called *sub*modalities, because they are the smaller elements within the five sensory modalities. (See Appendix, p. 203) I am going to pursue these submodality questions, both because I want to elicit her representation more completely, and because I also want the client to be consciously aware of these distinctions. Asking these questions also represents a sincere enquiry into the details of the client's experience, and therefore it's a respectful matching of her experience, something that Milton Erickson often emphasized.

GLT: "So, it is round, like a rock—tell me, is it hard or soft?" (Easy isn't it—this isn't rocket science.)

C: "Hard, very hard."

GLT: "And is it heavy or light?" (Go on, take a guess!)

C: "Heavy." Now, some people may be concerned at this point that I might be leading this client in the same way the therapist with the cancer group was doing. No, I am not. She has a rock in her throat, a rock! What I want her to be able to do is to *visualise* it and see it there as though seeing a rock in her throat is the most natural thing in the world. I don't tell her that her rock is dark or soft, or anything else; I *ask* her what *her* rock is like, and if she happened to have a chunk of pumice in her throat, it would have been light and soft, rather than heavy and hard.

So my client with the lump in her throat now has something more tangible than a simple kinaesthetic abstraction. She doesn't have just the sensation of a rock; now the representation has more qualities—weight and shape. So our therapist asks the next question:

GLT: "And if that rock were to have a colour, what colour would it have?" Notice the presupposition and bind here. She can't say, "It doesn't have a colour" because I am simply asking, *"If* it *were* to have a colour . . . "

C: "It's dark." This is fairly predictable; she's unlikely to say it's "light." "Heavy" things tend to be dark in colour and "light" things tend to be, well, *light*. I could ask more questions, such as "how big is it?" "Does it have movement?" "Does it have a background?" etc. At this point she can visualise it naturally and easily, and I'll start playing a little. I'll ask her, "What happens when you make it bigger?" "What happens when you make it darker?" etc., to see what change is created by each submodality shift.

This technique is nice for eliminating unwanted feelings, or enhancing desirable ones, depending on which way you shift the submodalities. It works wonderfully well on headaches, utilising the approach first suggested by Gestalt Therapists years ago. Basically the client visualises the headache appearing in a chair opposite them, develops a full and detailed image, and then transforms the qualities of the image in various ways until the headache is no longer felt.

This method is also very similar to the evocation technique of the occultists. Cast into the Triangle of Art, the representation is evoked and takes on a visible form that can be communicated with. The magician seeks to dominate this entity and to bring it under his magickal will. Most students of the Magickal Qabalah and of Chaos Magick will recognise the uncanny similarity of many NLP techniques with their own magical processes.

The semantic loading of language powerfully affects each person's interpretation of it differently. If you go up to a psychiatrist and ask him to hallucinate a spider in the palm of your outstretched hand, he is not likely to do that, because to those trained in psychiatry a "hallucination" is a thoroughly negative event to be avoided or medicated away. To a psychiatrist, a hallucination is a terrible thing that is likely to make someone jump off a tall building in the erroneous belief that they can fly.

However, to a hypnotist, the word "hallucinate" may only mean imagining something that isn't there. So, in asking someone to "hallucinate" a spider, you may not actually be asking them to do the thing that you thought you were. In NLP terms, "The meaning of your communication is the response that you get" is particularly pertinent here.

But if you stretch out your palm toward the psychiatrist and say, "*If* I were to have a spider in my hand, what sort of spider would it be?" you are more likely to get a congruent response. Then you can go on to ask what colour it is, how big it is, which way is it facing etc. Then—just for fun—move your hand toward him and watch for the reaction. If he doesn't like spiders, usually he will flinch or draw back quickly. Be sure to anchor this response—it might come in handy later on!

So you can imagine my alarm when I asked one schizophrenic lady what shape an unpleasant kinaesthetic feeling in her chest possessed.

"It is shaped like an aborted foetus," she said, and immediately started freaking out. With hindsight maybe "possessed" was not the best word to use! Now you can shift submodalities as much as you like, but whether it is large, small, in colour or black and white, focused or blurred, however you represent it—an aborted foetus is still an aborted foetus.

Now if we compare this to a rock, a "rock" is a fairly simple static event and a small rock is just a pebble. Neither carry much intrinsic emotional loading. However, an "aborted foetus" relates to a complex web of events which are invariably heavily emotionally laden, and whether it is small or large, colourful or black and white—it is still something with much the same meaning. I thus learned to avoid asking such questions too early on in my work with people experiencing psychotic symptoms.

One schizophrenic patient told me that his feeling looked like "the devil," and another told me his kinaesthetic was a "black hole" that was "sucking" him in. Just for the hell of it, I asked what would happen if he made it a *white* hole? He looked at me with disdain, informing me that black holes suck *everything* in, even light. I checked in a book, and of course he was quite right.

rock in throat   Submodalities] parts
___ shape = round
like a rock
hard
heavy
dark

Direct suggestions?

Heaviness

"If obesity is a disease, it is the only one that I am familiar with that you can cure by taking long walks and keeping your mouth shut."
—Rick Berman

When I first started out as a hypnotherapist, most of the clients I saw wanted to lose weight or stop smoking. Initially I was quite overwhelmed by the number of people who wanted help. Some were seeking what I term "cosmetic weight loss"—those who want to lose a few pounds in order to slip more easily into their bikini. Then there were the morbidly obese who would be unlikely to risk even setting foot on a beach in the first place.

So I quickly developed a filtering system to discriminate between these two groups. On the telephone I asked a simple question, "Do I need to fear for my furniture?"

Morbidly obese clients tend to be remarkably suggestible, and even today continue to be some of the best trance subjects I see. Student hypnotists and NLP practitioners wanting to gain experience in hypnosis would do well to start with them.

I began a little experiment with a group of five obese clients who agreed to help me out with a new approach, although they didn't know what this approach was going to be. In individual sessions I would quickly hypnotise the client into a deep and satisfactory trance, leave them for 40 minutes and then wake them up with the suggestion that they would be amnesic for the session. I would also suggest that the work undertaken during trance would continue to *operate deeply at an unconscious level.*

But in actual fact, in between the rapid trance induction, deepening suggestions and waking them up, I did and said *nothing at all!*

All five of these clients found that weekly sessions of this nature over a 10-week period proved to be highly beneficial. All these clients reduced down to their desired weight, and as one client put it, "The weight is just dropping off." Follow-up later at six and twelve months demonstrated that all five were stabilised at their desired weight, and that all had also found other interesting changes occurring in their lives, including an increase in daily physical activities rather than sedentary pastimes such as watching television.

Now how could I understand this strange success? It certainly wasn't due to the 40 minutes of not doing anything, so it must have been something about the trance induction. When I examined the standard suggestions and ambiguities that I had been utilising for the trance induction, some plausible possibilities emerged.

". . . and as you sit in the chair getting even more comfortable. . . . I want you to feel the weight of your body in the chair, . . . really feel that weight. . . ."

Many overweight people only notice their weight when they are moving, not when they are sitting still. Noticing their weight when still in front of the TV could elicit ongoing motivation to lose weight.

". . . and the longer you sit, the heavier you will feel, . . . and the longer you sit, the heavier you will feel . . . you are really heavy now."

If we assume that a suggestion like this will continue to operate unconsciously in everyday life, the longer they sit still, the heavier they will feel, and the more motivation they will have to do something about it.

". . . and as you sit heavily in the chair, you can hear the sound of my voice, and as you notice your body, you can begin to move your body in order to get more comfortable, move your body in any way possible for you to get a greater sense of comfort in your body by moving it. . . ."

That is a pretty direct suggestion that links the feeling of heaviness to physical activity.

Another result that I found interesting was that all these clients reported sleeping so much better, even though the sessions I ran amounted to little more than relaxation training. Recent studies by a number of research centres have found a strong correlation between poor sleep patterns and obesity. Studies found that people who regularly slept for five hours or less had 15% more of the hormone, ghrelin, which increases feelings of hunger. They were also found to have 15% less leptin, a hormone that suppresses appetite. Poor sleep affects these hormones, which in turn creates a disturbance in the regulation of appetite. This can lead to a circular process whereby the issues associated with being overweight can in turn disrupt what might otherwise be a normal sleep pattern. In light of this research, I now routinely examine the sleep patterns of obese clients and correct the insomnia issues that I commonly find.

Many obese clients talk in terms of being "addicted" to food. For many this may simply be a convenient expression; for others it may well be the truth. Brain imaging studies have demonstrated that the pleasure centres in the brains of cocaine addicts, alcoholics and heroin addicts "light up" when they see, or think about, their drug of choice. For some this effect will continue to occur even after years of abstinence. So examining the food addict's response to their "drug of choice" is also important.

However, the comparison of obesity with drug addiction is inappropriate for one simple and unfortunate reason—whilst the heroin addict and cocaine user can completely abstain from their drug and continue to live, the food addict still has to eat. Moreover, food is everywhere.

I have worked with a number of retired heroin addicts who want to quit smoking tobacco and many report the same thing—that giving up heroin was easy in comparison, because they can stay away from heroin fairly easily. For smokers, their drug of addiction is everywhere; it's hard to even buy a paper without seeing the cartons of drugs neatly lined up behind the counter. And deep within the neurology of a tobacco addict the crucial bit of their brain lights right up—*Ting!*—completely outside of their conscious control.

The food addict has quite the same problem; complete abstinence isn't an option, because they still *have* to eat, and food is everywhere. Advertising for food products is everywhere, and so are the supermarkets, fast food outlets, and so on. They all have carefully designed and expensive advertising, free gifts, enhanced flavours, super-sized portions, value meals and "happy" meals and so many gustatory delights, all creating that magical *Ting!* deep inside the neurology of the food addict.

Advertising is a powerful hypnotic process, and since we know that obese people are easily suggestible, they are particularly vulnerable. So whilst tackling the nature of a food addiction "head on" may be in order for some clients, some ego strengthening and inoculation against the widespread suggestions to *eat more* is probably in order for all obese clients.

Another problem is that there are a number of gustatory predicates and phrases that are common in everyday language, and these are constant reminders of eating. For example, a person considered a good judge of quality may be said to, "*have good taste*" or "*expensive taste*," and we may be reminded to *savor* our experience.

In addition, our language is filled with profound metaphors linking how we eat with how we take in and process information, and these are constant reminders of eating. Some teachers may complain that students want to be "*spoon fed*" information, and the flow of information from a news channel on TV is called a "*news feed.*" Someone who likes to take in information and then go away and think about it may want to "*chew the idea over*" and certainly wouldn't want it to be "*shoved down his throat.*" People who dwell on things, obsessively thinking about them, "*ruminate*" on those things, and whilst we are thinking of cows, when a new idea appears, some people will "*milk it*" for all it is worth.

The word "*gullible*" comes from the old English word "gull" which means both *swallow*, and also *a fool*. When we tell an outrageous lie to our boss, we may tell our colleagues, "*I cannot believe he swallowed that!*" Some keen students demonstrate a "*hunger for knowledge*" whilst others will quickly become "*fed up*" with their course.

Meanwhile, in working with anorexics, I find that much of their behaviour during therapy sessions is centered around refusing new information in much the same way that they refuse food. The anorexic will reject the reality of their skeletal frame as much as they'll reject that cake.

This food/information analogy also extends to bulimic patients, who are overly compliant, actively listening to every word that the therapist says and keen to fit in with the therapist's ideals. *Then*— much like leaving the dinner table to go to the bathroom and vomit— they leave the session and promptly regurgitate the lot. Newbie therapists easily miss this, and far too many are conned in this way by their bulimic clients. After my first session with a bulimic client I thought, "It can't be this easy, surely?" It wasn't.

Meanwhile, several colleagues have commented how overeaters don't really chew, taste, or savor their food. One result of this is that they don't get any feedback about when they have eaten enough. It is as if their overeating behaviour occurs in a trance-like state. So whilst the anorexic rejects food/information and the bulimic never really takes in the food/information, the overeater doesn't always consciously process what they are told, rendering them grossly susceptible to indirect hypnotic suggestions—regardless of whether they are delivered by a therapeutic hypnotist or a professional food-advertising agency.

The Television Set

"Doubt is to certainty as neurosis is to psychosis. The neurotic is in doubt and has fears about persons and things; the psychotic has convictions and makes claims about them. In short, the neurotic has problems, the psychotic has solutions." —Thomas Szasz

One man I worked with appeared to believe that he was a television set. In taking his history I learned that his father had subjected him to a psychological profiling when he was 13, in order to establish what sort of person he was going to be. Thus armed with the results of his paper and pencil test, this man thought that he knew his son better than the son knew himself. From that day, a gulf between them grew steadily. This man never actually spoke to his *son*—he spoke to the ghost he had created some 20 years earlier with that *damned* pencil and paper test.

My client, a paranoid schizophrenic, told me, "Whenever I am with him, I feel like I am a badly-tuned TV set." Naturally I asked him which channel he was tuned into, to which he replied, "That's just it; I don't know. Whatever channel I'm on, Dad seems to be watching something else. He never sees *me*."

I often have clients who report that their parents hardly know the "real" them at all—it is as though the person the parent speaks to is someone else entirely, and any response the child gives that doesn't fit the expectation is simply ignored or corrected. From these parents I hear things such as, "I know my child better than my child knows himself" and other such misguided thinking. For a more esoteric and detailed description of this experience see R. D, Laing's *The Politics of Experience* (29) and *Sanity, Madness and the Family.* (31)

Richard Bandler suggests that when someone asks socially, "So, what do you do?" asking about your job, the chances are that they are seeking to relate to you in any way other than to the human being in front of them. We tend to look for the "hook"—the commonality by which we think we may know a little of the other person. When someone says to me, "You know, you really remind me of my father/brother/someone-back-home," they are really relating to that other person, rather than to me, the person here in front of them.

So now here's the irony. The schizophrenic feels that his parents don't see *him*, they only see their *image* of him, which according to the schizophrenic is a gross distortion. But according to the parents, it is the *son's image of himself* that is in error—after all, the pencil and paper test says so. So he goes to hospital and is given a diagnosis, which means that nobody else there sees *him* either. They just see the "schizophrenic," or the "patient," or whatever role is assigned by the institution.

With enough psychotropic drugs, he starts to fade away and sooner or later he risks even losing himself. But it's OK—everyone maintains his rights *as a mental health patient,* and behaves professionally toward him—even if they do fail to see exactly what is there right in front of their nose—a suffering and unrecognized human being.

This seems a reasonable juncture to say a little bit about "professional boundaries." Given many of my antics, I frighten a lot of professionals. I have received complaints that it is grossly "unprofessional" to take long-term institutionalised schizophrenics to biker's pubs and gothic nightclubs. Naturally my response is to ask, "Which nightclubs would you prefer me to take them to?"—a response that many professionals might describe as "tangential" or even "schizophrenic." The issue at hand for these people appears to be about when my personal behavior conflicts with my professional behavior. Here's the deal—it's about personal congruency. If you were 100% congruent in your beliefs and behaviours, why would you *ever* need to hide behind "professional boundaries"?

Incongruence in psychiatric professionals all too often results from a conflict between their personal and professional lives. This is never helpful to schizophrenics, who have the hardest time dealing with *any* form of incongruence. If you want to observe professional incongruence, go and ask the prescribing psychiatrist, "Will these drugs give me tardive dyskinesia?" and watch him squirm. (Tardive dyskinesia is a serious and chronic movement disorder caused by the drugs that lower dopamine levels—those used to treat schizophrenia.)

If you are a therapist, it is worth noting that many "symptoms" associated with modern madness are actually only side effects of the drugs, so it is well worth familiarising yourself with these. During my days as a nursing student, I attended a psychopharmacology lecture where the lecturer was waxing eloquent about the benefits of neu-roleptic medications. "They enable seriously mentally patients to live normal lives," he told us. I asked if we could all try one drug each for a week in order to experience how they worked for ourselves. He said no, because he believed that would be far too dangerous—but apparently not dangerous enough to prevent the wholesale drugging of those regarded as mentally ill or "chemically imbalanced."

Go ask the psychiatric occupational therapist, "Will patting this balloon around really make me sane?" and again, watch for the signs of discomfort.

When I answer a question, I answer it congruently, not according to the rules of the institution, or a "professional role." Let's get real and stop hiding behind policy.

A Therapeutic Relationship

"Sex without love is an empty experience,
but, as empty experiences go, it's one of the best."
—Woody Allen

Relationships sure can be funny things. Two people meet and quickly start trying to turn the other person into someone else. I once heard a psychotherapist say that it's strange that when two people commit to each other, they quickly cease to do the very things that attracted the other person to them in the first place. A case in point was the short-lived marital bliss of a colleague of mine. Shortly after returning from the honeymoon, the wife said to me, "I am married now, I no longer need to try." I wasn't quite sure what it was exactly that she didn't need to try any more, but unsurprisingly the relationship lasted only six weeks. The husband is living with the best man now; it's funny how some things turn out.

Another friend, a stoical scientist, went to relationship counselling with her husband to see if they could resolve their troublesome issues. "Is it working?" I asked her one day. "Hell yes!" she said enthusiastically, "I now know more than ever that I have to *divorce* that son-of-a-bitch." Somehow she seemed disappointed that they weren't doing therapy with the foam bats where you repeatedly hit your spouse to vent all your anger.

Now we know that this type of "cathartic therapy" is just plain stupid. All it does is teach the person to be more angry, more often, let it move into more overt violence, and then expect praise for it. There's an absurd belief amongst therapists that depression is caused by "anger turned inwards"—so they teach their depressives to vent their anger towards others through cathartic techniques. All that creates is a bunch of angry depressives—not necessarily an improvement.

One story I read recently turned out differently. It seemed that the therapy was working, but the wife needed more and more sessions, mostly without her husband being there. Poor guy, it took him over a year to work it out. He was paying sixty pounds for every 50-minute hour that the therapist was screwing his wife. She eventually took the house, the kids and the rabbit and shacked up with the counsellor. And I don't think the guy got a refund.

"Yo-Yo" Dieting

"Diets, like clothes, should be tailored to you."
—Joan Rivers

Recently I saw a T-shirt in a shop window with the statement, "Quitting is for Losers" printed on it. As I walked on, I wondered about the motivational consequences of those words before passing a rather obese man smoking a cigarette, walking in the other direction— wearing the same shirt.

This got me thinking about "weight loss" and "giving up" smoking. Both phrases have connotations of the loss of something valuable; not something many people enjoy. Many people try "losing weight" and "giving up" harmful habits for a while, and then soon go back to their more familiar behaviours.

By the time an overweight person seeks psychotherapy to overcome their problems they are usually desperate to try *anything* that might work. They will often have tried every diet fad, taken herbal remedies, tried acupuncture, colonic irrigation, taken their life in their hands with ear candling or whatever. The level of desperation can be really very high.

In fact, many troubled overeaters will do just about *anything* to get away from their weight issues. The motivation tends to be *"I don't want to be fat,"* and the emotional value attributed to the motivation is often "I *hate* being like this," or some other unpleasant negative feeling. So their strategy for change itself tends to produce a powerfully negative state.

In terms of NLP meta-programs, the client will usually have "away from" motivation, and there will tend to be a lack of any realistic "towards" goals. They know what they *don't* want, but they rarely really know what it is that they *do* want.

Someone who is morbidly obese may desire weight loss not

50

because they want to move _toward_ something positive, but because they are moving "away from" obesity and/or any resulting problems. The absence of a positive goal to go *toward* presents a problem, because as weight is lost, the level of motivation decreases proportionally. As they feel less fat, they are less inclined to be motivated about losing more weight or maintaining a weight loss, so the weight increases again. As the person regains weight to a level where the motivation to move "away from" obesity is triggered, the cycle starts again.

However, repeated exposure to the triggers of the "away from" motivation also results in a form of systematic desensitization; the away from motivation at a given weight becomes less intense over time, so more weight is required to achieve the same intensity of motivation to lose weight.

The same is often true of any other yo-yo pattern of quitting any other behavior. This is probably why yo-yo dieters, cigarette quitters, alcoholics and gamblers who are always quitting, tend to demonstrate an increase in the problem behaviour over time and are able to tolerate levels of the problem that would *terrify* anyone else.

There is another serious problem with motivation based on unpleasant feelings; they will tend to go *away* from all those everpresent bad feelings. No wonder they will opt to cheer themselves up with some fizzy drink, cake, or a gorgeous plate of chips.

Put under a bit of pressure, the overweight client will often state a "towards" value—or at least, a value that *sounds* like a "towards" value. They will say something like, "I want to look and weigh what I did when I was 27 years old," or "I want to be as I was on my wedding day." However this "towards" value, or goal, is invariably historically based. When you examine an obese client's timeline and the position of their goal, invariably you will find their goal is located firmly in their *past*. Now think about that. How is it possible to move towards something that is based in the *past*?

So in building goals for them to move toward, it is important to make sure it is in their future. Their outcome is *not* to return to how they looked in the past, but rather to move forward to how they will look, feel and *be* a year from now *in the future*!

Another problem is the associations that a client may have to being their ideal weight. I have found it very useful to ask an overweight client the following question: *"What happened at the time that you were last at your desired weight?"*

At one weight loss seminar with 14 overweight participants, 13 of them expressed surprise when I asked this question. For each of these 13 there had indeed been a serious stress or traumatic event at that time. For one, there was a bereavement, another was assaulted, another was made redundant and wondered if at her age she'd ever get another job, another got married to a man who turned out to be controlling and abusive, and so on. All but one had a unique story of trauma or stress that had been paired with being at their ideal weight. The result of this is an equivalence: "ideal weight equals trauma," and understandably this detracts from their motivation to reach their ideal weight. Resolving the client's reactions to the traumatic past event can have a dramatic influence on their congruent motivation to reach a normal weight.

Yet another pattern to watch out for is the person who wants that "final cigarette" or "one last donut" or "one last flutter on the horses" before they begin change work. The yo-yo quitter and the addict will often be found outside the therapist's office indulging in "one last" episode of their addiction. On entering the office, the motivation for indulgence is largely absent, because the desire has just been satisfied. The therapy occurs in a state in which the driver for the problem is absent, so it can't really be addressed. The client leaves the office with the therapist satisfied that the client has changed, when s/he hasn't. I did a quick survey last year of smokers who had seen hypnotherapists, but carried on smoking afterwards, despite an apparently successful session, and this pattern was true of them all.

Of those smokers who had successfully quit following hypnotherapy, *none* had smoked from between the time they woke up to their appointment with the therapist. They all entered the session in a state of craving, so it could become part of the process of change.

As one psychiatrist told me, "Alcoholics only want to quit drinking when they are drunk; when they are sober all they want is another drink." This principle seems to apply well across contexts and different addictions.

Endless Loops

"There is no absurdity so palpable but that it may be firmly planted in the human head if you only begin to inculcate it before the age of five, by constantly repeating it with an air of great solemnity."
—Arthur Schopenhauer

A few years ago a Japanese chap named Aki Maita made toy manufacturer *Bandai* a fortune by designing a little egg-shaped devise called a "cyber-pet" that ran a simple program. Without external intervention (the owner pressing one of several buttons in response to a little cheeping noise) this program was *designed to fail*. Some of these little creatures contained a sub-routine in their program so that after a certain passage of time, the sad cheeping of the dying pet would increase in speed and thus help create a sense of urgency in the owner—or probably the owner's parent, who couldn't stand it any longer. If the program failed for long enough then the devise would shut down and "die."

Soon, well-trained human consumers all across the world were pressing little buttons to the command of these electronic devises. Children cried when their little pet no longer let out a little "cheep" to let them know that it needed "feeding," an indication that it had died. Other children were left confused as to why they were not allowed to own one, too. All of this highly lucrative lunacy occurred within a description that these little electronic gadgets were "pets," and that the cute little cheeping noises were "communication" that indicated that it needed "feeding" or "exercising," and that pressing one of the little buttons was meeting this need. All this framing made this behaviour not only acceptable, but for many people, *compulsory*. I wonder how all of this would look to an alien doing his Masters in human anthropology?

Most computer programs are not deliberately designed to expire without human intervention, yet it was this very feature that appeared

53

to fulfill a strong need in a great many people. I guess the term "pet" was correct—this is the situation that faces any animal that we have turned into our pet. Without our intervention on a regular basis, the creature will expire because we deliberately make them dependent on ourselves. It brings us pleasure to see the gratitude on their little faces when we meet the needs that they would meet for themselves in their natural environment.

This is creepy.

It kind of reminds me of psychiatry.

Obsessions and Compulsions

"The significant problems that we face cannot be solved by the same level of thinking that created them." —Albert Einstein

Obsessive-compulsive disorder (OCD) presents the NLP Practitioner with an interesting challenge, especially if the client has previously received unsuccessful therapy. Psychiatry is ever-increasingly suggesting biological reasons for "mental disease," and more and more often I hear clients suggest that they believe that they are genetically predisposed to their particular problem. Increased awareness and interest in Tourette's Syndrome, a neurological disorder that includes obsessions and rituals similar on the surface to OCD, is encouraging the psychiatric industry to investigate the neurological basis of OCD further. Even if this might be true, none of this appears to benefit the clients who have explored the psychiatric route for OCD "treatment," madication. (The first time I used the term, "madication" several people wrote to me to point out the supposed typographical error. I do make such errors, but this isn't one of them.)

While the psychiatrist views the OCD patient as suffering from a biochemical disorder for which he needs to madicate, the CBT nurse will attempt a behavioural modification program, while the Freudian prefers to analyse the patient's subconscious. In all cases the person is perceived as being "ill" and in need of "treatment"— whether that includes an eclectic approach including counselling, madication and CBT, or the old solution, lobotomy.

What all these approaches miss is that people suffering from OCD are caught in a never-ending loop with no exit. This is what computer programmers call a *software* problem, rather than a hardware problem. An otherwise functional computer programmed with an endless loop cycles endlessly (and uselessly), something programmers take great pains to avoid. For instance, an obsessive-compulsive client I saw could never leave the house without checking all the plugs, sockets, gas knobs, etc., many times over. Finally she'd leave the house, only to have to quickly return just in case that in checking the appliances she had inadvertently switched something back on again! She could only abandon her checking strategy when the guilt of keeping her husband waiting, or her fear of being late once again for work, or some other external force pulled her *out* of the checking strategy and *into* her "guilt" strategy. She was in a lose/lose game in which one obsessive strategy could only be exited by attending to a more urgent obsession, leaving her feeling seriously bad.

When most people leave their house, they may check the stove, turn out the lights and check the locks, *once*—or perhaps *twice*. Having done that, they go on to other activities. If you ask them if they have locked the door, they will quickly make a clear image of having done that, and confidently reply "Yes." OCD clients apparently are not able to do this, so they continue to check, endlessly, and find it almost impossible to go on to something else. If you think about a time when you weren't sure whether you had locked a door or not, you can find out what was lacking in your memory at that time.

Some have suggested that an OCD sufferer may be so attentive to an anxious internal voice that they can't attend to the remembered images that would convince them that they had already done what they need to do. This is something that I plan to check out at the first opportunity.

If they continue to check in the external world, they are called compulsive, and if they only do it in their minds, they are called obsessive. Some lucky ones do both, until an injection, external restraint, or some other external force diverts their strategy. Having seen it first hand, I can assure you that no external force is faster or more efficient in interrupting an endless loop than an 80-volt shock to the temporal lobes down in the ECT rooms.

The astute NLP Practitioner will take a different approach, and create an *exit* point in the compulsive behavioural loop. For instance, a typical example of OCD occurs in "speed freaks"—the guys who live fast and play fast. I have met a number of highly driven and successful cocaine users. One client in particular consulted me with a concern that he was unlikely to live beyond the age of forty owing to his lifestyle. He was at least somewhat aware of his lack of internal control.

"How do you know when to stop?" I asked him, as he sat there twitching as if he was revved up on adrenaline and stimulants.

"Stop what?" He replied quickly, a revealing response.

"Anything? Just give me an example of something you do that you know *when* to stop doing it."

As we started sorting through different scenarios, a consistent pattern emerged. He'd only stop a night of taking cocaine when he'd run out of the drug, was unable to get more of it, had collapsed physically, or had run out of money. He'd drink alcohol until unconsciousness set in. When working on a project, he'd only stop when it was finished, taken away from him, or when he'd collapse with fatigue. When driving, he'd drive as fast as he could until he was stopped by traffic, road conditions, or pulled over by the police. The consistent pattern was that to stop doing anything demanded an external force that was greater than his internal desire. At that point he began to realise how he was stuck.

The other pattern was that all his decision strategies were driven by internal representations that were associated *still* pictures rather than movies. This meant that he was always in the moment, and never "thought things through" to see the possible future consequences of his decisions or behaviours.

Back in the 1960s many people who were caught up in obsessively thinking about the past or the future—or both—wanted to "be in the now," without having the faintest idea of what that might entail. This guy was definitely in the now, but that didn't work very well for him. Many Alzheimer's patients are quite thoroughly in the "now" because their ability to remember the past and forecast the future are gone, but most people don't find that particularly appealing.

By getting him to turn his still pictures into *movies* of what happens next, and what happens after that, and so on, he was able to begin to see the consequences that would occur. When he saw those consequences, he easily made different decisions. Step-by-step I took him through a number of these movies until it became a generalised ability. With this broader time perspective, he was able to have more of a future-based orientation, rather than being stuck in the moment and his need for immediate gratification. An OCD client may seem very different, but they have the same inability to stop, and they, too, need an exit.

Equivalence

"Two determined ambulance men went to the wrong address, grabbed a healthy Norwegian, slapped him onto a stretcher and rushed him to a hospital in Kragero, 40 miles away, despite his vociferous objections. Meanwhile the real patient, who had the same name and lived in the same village, despite suffering from severe anaemia, drove himself to the hospital, where he had problems registering because the clerk insisted he was already there."
—Fortean Times

As I worked with clients, I began to notice the importance of the *equivalences* they expressed. It's an obvious observation really, one that has probably already been described elsewhere, but I was pleased to have discovered it. For instance, one woman came to me expressing concern over the anxiety she felt when she considered a forthcoming job interview. The job was one in which she would attain a promotion, work less hours, and earn more money. As she described it, it was a *dream job*.

"So, what's the problem?" I asked.

"Well, when I think about the interview, rather than the job, it feels like I am going to an execution," she said nervously.

"Hmmm. *Your* execution?" I asked, reaching for my pad.

Now, I thought to myself, an execution is not really equivalent to a job interview; these things are just *not* the same. Curious, I elicited the submodalities of her execution (which was a hanging by the way, for the Freudians out there who just *have* to know these things), and wrote them down. Unsurprisingly, when I elicited the submodalities of the job interview, they were the same. She was dissociated from both pictures, which were panoramic, and they were three-dimensional movies that only played halfway, without conclusion. Needless to say, neither were particular bright and colourful. In

58

fact both were described as "dark" and "gloomy." That made me wonder if all complex equivalencies are coded with the same submodalities? Is that how they are made "equal," so that they *feel the same*"?

When a psychiatrist assumes that someone's discomfort is a result of a chemical imbalance, they are making the same kind of equivalence: "client's problem" = "chemical imbalance."

Quite often a client will begin discussing the *physical* nature of their problem and express concern about the return of their symptoms once they "come off" medication. Their equivalence is, "no medication = return of symptoms." The astute NLP Practitioner will notice how this client has unwittingly pre-planned for the return of their symptoms, by coding it on their future timeline. Naturally, most people will equate a return of a symptom as an indication of failure, but this can also be changed.

A common strategy of therapists such as Milton Erickson and Jay Haley was to deliberately program a relapse of the symptoms. For instance, having worked quite successfully with a young lady with a bed-wetting problem, I told her in trance that I wanted her to have an occasional relapse over the next month or two, and that she was to have *at least three* relapses before really knowing that her problem was well and truly in the past. That redefined a relapse as a result of my suggestion, and that she would need *three* such relapses to know that the treatment was successful. "Three relapses = success" is a lot different than "One relapse = failure" which is what most people would otherwise assume. When a relapse is future-paced appropriately in this way, then a return of the symptom will be a confirmation of the *success* of the treatment, rather than an indication of failure. A planned relapse also gives the client an opportunity for dealing with the problem themselves in response to what they have learned.

Predicting relapses has several other interesting features. It takes some of the pressure off the client to be 100% successful—which is particularly helpful with a perfectionist. And it allows the therapist to indirectly appear to exert control over the symptoms. It also demonstrates that symptoms don't "*just happen,*" as so many clients believe, and gives the client an opportunity to apply their own unconscious resolution to the problem. *They* are the one who begins to "drive the bus," in contrast to being driven by their symptoms, or having the therapist provide the solution or panacea.

Hoarding

With some clients I make a point of visiting at home prior to working with them. One client had one of the most serious set of OCD rituals I have ever witnessed, revolving around a fixation about losing things. She could never throw anything away, lest she lose something of value. I had to ask the natural question, "Did she actually have anything valuable to lose?" Of course, considering her lifestyle and resulting lack of income, she didn't. Her life was so dominated by this strategy that she was unable to work and consequently lived on welfare.

She was taking prescribed Paroxetine (an SSRI), lorazepam (a tiny but potent little tranquilizer) and sulpiride (an old drug formerly used by psychiatrists for drugging schizophrenics). This powerful pharmacological cocktail had made no difference whatsoever in her problem. She was unkempt, smelt bad, was highly anxious, looked eccentric (read "batshit crazy") and was socially isolated. A few years previously she had been hospitalised after a complaint by neighbours had lead to the Environmental Health Team visiting her house. A concern was raised to the mental health team, which briefly hospitalised and madicated her while her house was excavated and steam-cleaned.

When I visited her house, it was brimming with junk and rubbish. Since the trip to the funny farm, nothing had ever been thrown away. Her bath, shower, and sinks all had little sieves to filter the water, in case something might drop off and be flushed away. Washing was hard for her, owing to the anxiety it generated. On top of her bathroom cabinet, she had several little jars full of fluff, which turned out to be from her belly button. She couldn't even throw that out, because while discarding it she might accidentally throw away something of value.

Waste disposal and hygiene were coded as a complex equivalence with *loss*. Now it seems to me that these things are most definitely *not* equal, but this woman's right cerebral hemisphere didn't know that.

Sometimes these clients are grieving over a significant personal loss that they are stuck in, and that has generalized and persisted. After losing someone significant, they don't want to take the *slightest* chance of losing anything else. Steve and Connirae Andreas' NLP Grief Resolution process (5) can be valuable in clearing up such issues.

With this particular client, there were three more questions I naturally wanted to know the answers to:

1. "What happens when she uses the toilet?"

2. "How would she know if she *didn't* throw something of value away?"

3. "How would she know if she *had* indeed thrown something of value away?"

Her strategy was simple and global: discarding *any* object/item was equivalent to losing something of value. She had no criteria for deciding what actually constituted an item of value. When an old empty milk carton is equivalent in value to a gold coin, it can go one of two ways. Either the gold coin is as worthless as the old empty milk carton, or the carton is as valuable as the gold. She didn't have a threshold within her strategy that would enable her to exit her loop.

Another client had presupposed in her OCD checking strategy that she would have to check something 12, 24, or 36 times in order to know that the door was in fact locked, or the gas was actually turned off. As a result she had lots of little rituals arranged in her life, and her colleagues at work viewed her as "rather eccentric." Here is what I wanted to know—what happened to the submodalities of her representation on the 12th, 24th, or 36th time that *didn't* happen on the one before (or after) that, which enabled her to exit her strategy? Whatever it was would be the difference that made the difference.

This woman *was* able to competently exit her loop when she took a shit, so she *did* possess a strategy for disposing of unwanted waste that didn't produce anxiety for her—albeit just once or twice a week. This was all that was necessary in order to build a new set of generalisations for her, and a new strategy for living. This took about 5 sessions in total—the actual change probably only took a few minutes, it just took me all that time to discover the right way of packaging the solution.

frame setting

Learning

"If we continually try to force a child to do what he is afraid to do,
he will become more timid, and will use his brains and energy,
not to explore the unknown, but to find ways to avoid the
pressures we put on him."   —John Holt *How Children Learn*

One trap many students fall into is that they incorporate *new* information into their *old* understanding. For instance, "Electrons orbit around the nucleus of an atom, just the way the planets revolve around the sun." The framework of understanding something is already in place, and it is used for new content, whether that is appropriate or not. Sometimes this is a "force fit" that does considerable violence to the new information.

All too often in seminars, I hear someone say, "Oh, what you are saying is just like X, Y, Z" when in fact what I am saying is nothing of the sort. When I hear statements like this, I realize that I have not used effective enough frame-setting in order to nest the information into the right context for the listener.

When people attempt to acquire new information in this way, they often fail to expand and enrich their model of the world. Instead, they only reinforce their pre-existing conceptions. In training, this is something that you may want your listeners to avoid doing if you want to teach them something new.

On a sensory level we can presuppose that when two items have differing *content* (left hemisphere), but the *relationship* (right hemisphere) between the person and the items is the same, they will be codified with the same submodalities.

One problem is that teachers don't realize that in addition to the content that they are teaching, they need to *market* it and *present* it in a way that makes it appealing and easy to learn.

Like an advertiser, one of a teacher's tasks is to get the potential customer to codify the product with a submodality set that feels good. One method is to tell the customer to codify the product with V, X, Y, Z submodalities. "This is a BIG improvement upon the existing models and can really add COLOUR to your understanding." But somehow I suspect that this won't always work too well. The other method is to create a desirable state and anchor the product to it. This is easy and all too commonly observed in advertising: Show something sexy with the product, either simultaneously or sequentially.

Advertisers have known about this for years, but teachers and lecturers tend to quite unwittingly often do the reverse. They often create boredom and pain and attach it to the subject being taught. Then when the student remembers the subject, they feel bad again. Of course the simplest solution to this is to not remember the subject at all. From my work with teachers, I have observed a great disparity between what a teacher thinks s/he is teaching and what is actually being learned by their students.

During my brief time working for the army, I noticed how much the relationships between people in the military are dictated by the organisation itself. Various visual cues exist in the uniforms, insignia, and most importantly, saluting, and other rituals, so that everyone knows their relationship to everyone else, even if they are total strangers. The rigorous army discipline and ritual held these relationships mostly constant. Thus a corporal meeting an officer for the first time already knows a significant portion of the analogical relationship between him and the officer.

One result of this is that many army personnel were fantastic hypnotic subjects. It didn't take long before I was introduced to people as "This is Andrew; watch out, he's a hypnotist!" which set some very useful frames for me. On first meeting me, one woman shook my hand while staring at me in fear. When I let go, she remained frozen in space in a deep hypnotic state. Yet I had not done anything intentionally to create this.

The presuppositions arising from the way we were introduced to each other meant that as a hypnotist I must have some sort of strange power, and she codified our encounter as in some way a hypnotic one. *I* was saying hello, *she* was going into trance—because of the frame set by being introduced to a hypnotist. Stage hypnotist and

NLP Trainer, Paul McKenna suggests that the banner that states "HYPNOTIC STAGE SHOW" acts as the strongest presupposition of all when doing stage hypnosis shows.

One client who consulted me was having difficulty in many areas of his life. The recurring theme was that he tried to create the *same* relationship with *different* people in *different* contexts. For example, he regarded his employees as his "family" and treated his employees the same way that he would his own children or spouse. Of course, the downside of this was that his family often found themselves being treated as though they were employees in his organization. The relationships he tried to build were incongruent with the context in which the relationships were forged, and he found that very few people treated him with the respect that he wanted. He remained confused, since to "treat everyone the same way" was a criterion he held high, but this was not necessarily a value shared by everyone else.

A question I toyed with for some time was, "Just when does a submodality become *content*?" For example, if you have a representation of a small classroom with a very large whiteboard, the whiteboard itself lends both content and submodality representation. If we compare this to a representation of a small classroom with a very large *black*board what would we need to do to make both representations have identical submodalities?

When I first started using the swish pattern (during which time I went swish pattern crazy) I initially used a content swish—as I had been taught to do by a self-professed "NLP Trainer." In this technique one preferred picture bursts its way through the undesired picture, without any attention paid to the submodalities of either one. (I didn't actually know about submodalities then.) For example, a client's representation of an emotionally traumatic event was "swished" for something pleasant. I found this produced immediate effects but they were short-lived, and some clients would return later complaining of feeling worse.

It took me some months to realize what I was actually doing to these people. Since the relationship to the representation is established by the submodalities, shifting content can leave the original submodalities intact. With the swish pattern, the brain is triggered to go,

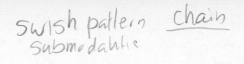

"Not that, *this!*" So following a content swish—which is really only a *chain*, not a swish—the following sequence can occur: The person thinks of the problem state with which they have a certain undesirable relationship, or feeling. This relationship is left unaddressed, and the brain swishes rapidly to the new representation, but sometimes carrying the same relationship/submodality set. The result of this is that when the client switches to something else (a neutral or resourceful representation) they *feel* the same way. An example of this effect is evident in another amusing story from the Fortean Times:

> After three days of uninterrupted heavy metal music from the flat next door, Gunthwilde Blom, 63, of Klagenfurt, Austria, began to get cross. She hammered on the walls and put notes under the door of the offending flat. All this had no effect so she confronted her neighbour, Wilma Kock, directly. Kock protested her innocence, but Blom did not believe her, calling her a "venomous herring." When the noise continued, Mrs Blom finally went berserk and pushed 20 lbs of fresh herring through her neighbour's letter-box. Ms. Kock called the police, who discovered while interviewing Blom that the music was actually coming from a radio she had inadvertently left on beneath her own bed. Unrepentant, she declared, "They didn't understand; Kock's a cow."

Imagine standing in a concert hall. The conductor is on vacation. At one end are some players playing their instruments out of harmony with one another. A couple of them might even be playing completely out of tune, and at a totally different volume from the rest. The sound is terrible and gives you a bit of a headache. So, rather than *tuning* them up and bringing them into harmony, you place a beat-box at the other end of the hall and crank it up so loud that you drown out the orchestra. That effectively puts the awful orchestra into the background, but the orchestra still plays badly—and now they play in competition with the beat-box.

The submodalities of the spoken words of the hypnotist will also act as the submodality drivers of the listener's representational systems. Given the way submodalities reflect the person's real world experiences, congruence is vital. For example in the real world "out there" how often does a human have the experience of an object moving farther away and getting bigger? While creating submodality shifts such as this can give rise to some pretty interesting states, incongruent voice tones are not likely to lead to success. For example, encouraging someone to begin to quieten their internal dialogue while shouting, or telling them to go deeper into trance with a rising pitch, may not result in the desired outcome, because the listener has to choose between responding to the digital words or the tone, one of the analogical aspects of the communication.

However, incongruencies in presentation can sometimes provide an interesting experience. Consider Ayres Rock in Australia. Long steeped in mystical significance, and admired by thousands of visitors, viewing it at dawn or dusk can provide an experience that few people forget. The Taj Mahal in Agra, India, also provides a spectacular sight when seen in dimming sunlight. Seeing the Taj made me wonder just how seldom we get to experience this particular combination of submodality shifts in the outside world, and whether when we do we might easily attribute something magical or mystical to it? For example, maybe our relationship to that external thing cannot be categorized into something that we are already familiar with from our internal mapping strategies. Inevitably it becomes something else. It is new in both its digital content and analogical presentation.

If this is the case then maybe the uniqueness of the experience is due to the "submodality set" that is unique to that particular experience—i.e. we cannot form a complex equivalence from it; we cannot easily say, "Oh yes, that big rock, when the sun goes down, it's just like the one I have in my back yard."

Core Transformation

"A donkey with a load of holy books is still a donkey."
—Traditional Sufi

While I was doing some client work in Johannesburg, South Africa, a phone call came through telling me that a client was being brought to me in a state of serious distress. She had been becoming increasingly withdrawn and irrational over the previous weeks, was eating very little, and had been hitting and cutting herself. A friend of hers had heard that I was in town. Frightened by what the South African psychiatric services would do to her, he decided to bring her to me as the first port of call. This lady, a disheveled and screeching 30-year-old who looked more like a 70-year-old, was quite literally dragged into my office by four men. She was unceremoniously dumped onto the couch where she immediately started hissing at me like a cornered and rabid cat.

I hissed back, and with my hands in a claw shape, scratched at the air in front of her face—to the utter bewilderment of the men who had brought her there. We hissed at each other for a few minutes before I started to calm down a bit and she followed.

"Enough?" I asked, "Or should we continue for a bit longer?" She gave me a half smile. "It is not easy, is it?" I continued, "Being you, I mean," and she nodded. I continued with gentle questioning, validating her reality, pacing and leading for nearly three hours until she was conversing nearly normally. Brief therapy this wasn't.

Having maneuvered her into a position where I could work with her, I outlined the Core Transformation process (3) to her. I would ask her hurting "part" the questions, and she could tell me the responses, *even if they made no sense to her whatsoever*. She agreed.

Her hurting part turned out to be an image of a "demon"—for want of a better description. This demon followed her everywhere

67

she went and tormented her endlessly. Gaining consent for co-operation from this demon was easy enough—it agreed to co-operate since it was completely sure that nothing would really work anyway. I ignored this expression of disbelief and proceeded.

In many NLP books, and listening to many NLP trainers, the impression is often given that all NLP-oriented sessions go rather magically. The reality is that they don't always go so well, or so quickly. So while I was expecting *some* change, I wasn't expecting an absolute change. But by the end of the process, she looked as though she'd seen God—I could almost hear the angels singing myself, and for a brief moment I was scared that maybe I'd just flipped her psychosis into a pseudo-religious ecstasy. Her physical appearance was dramatically different; she looked a *lot* younger than she did when she was dragged in, and even looked a few years younger than her physical age.

"Wow!" she said as she opened her eyes.

"Impressive huh?" I said, pretending to be nonchalant, and seriously regretting not having videotaped the session.

"Wow! I'm hungry," she said, her voice back to normal now. "No, I'm not. I'm really, *really* hungry! Got any food?" And at that, I knew the session was complete.

The Brain Hemispheres

*"If the human brain were so simple that we could understand it,
we would be so simple that we couldn't."*   —Lyall Watson

I often hear people say, "Well no one really knows how the brain works, do they?" and "Of course, we only ever use 10% of our brains anyway." I find that the people who say these things are usually those who have never read a neurology book or studied the subject.

The brain is divided up by anatomists in various ways. One division that most people are familiar with is that of the two hemispheres. Make two fists, and put them together. That is approximately the size of your brain. Each fist is one hemisphere. I'm sorry if you have small hands. It is worth noting that these two hemispheres have *contra-lateral* control. What this means is that the left half of the brain senses and controls the *right side* of the body and vice-versa.

While this contra-lateral control could be considered a universal norm, anyone working in neurosurgery for any length of time will have seen striking exceptions to this. As ever-greater successes in neurosurgery occur, and more people survive what would previously have been considered fatal brain damage, we are finding out more and more about how wrong our neurological generalisations can be. For example, I once had an 8-year-old patient who had lost almost the entire left hemisphere of his brain following a serious traffic accident. He made a full recovery without paralysis, loss of language, or any apparent cognitive impairment. As his greatly relieved mother commented, "He was always a bit of an oddball like that anyway!"

Here's a current list of the general functions of the *left* hemisphere:

Control of the right side of body.
Dominant perception, production of language and non-
    emotional expression.

Reading, writing, spelling, speaking, rules of grammar
   and syntax.
Sense of time.
Rhythm.
Small chunk information-processing.

So in the broadest sense, the left hemisphere is the hemisphere of conscious digital communication. This is true for the *majority* of people—most exceptions tend to occur in women and left-handed or ambidextrous people—and even more often in left-handed or ambidextrous women.

I nursed one patient who had received a nasty injury to the left hemisphere of his brain and consequently lost the use of his right arm and leg. The right side of his face also drooped slightly, but this improved with time, whereas the leg and arm did not.

Characteristically for a left-brain injured person, he became *aphasic* (He couldn't produce words). He was only able to utter a single syllable, "*fuck,*" and this could only be expressed during times of very strong emotions—typically frustration or anger. Of course there was plenty of opportunity for serious frustration for anyone plunged into the problems of semi-paralysis and mutism.

So why could this patient only communicate via "fuck" while he was in an *emotional* state? Because some of the generalised functions of the right hemisphere of the brain are:

Control of the left side of the body.
Auditory tone, timbre.
Emotions.
Pressured Speech/Baby talk.
Sexual drives.
Big chunk information processing ("the big picture"
   or gestalt).

Patients in this position are often reduced to single syllable communication, and the syllables often express terms of an emotional, aggressive, or sexual nature.

Thus the gentleman's communication range was reduced to: "Fuck fuck, . . . fuck *fuckfuckfuck*!!!!"

The staff of the rehabilitation centre soon attuned their ears to hearing the variation of pitch, tone, speed, volume, duration, etc. and assigned meaning to this essentially *analogical* communication. Mothers of newborn babies do this instinctively. Being preverbal, the infant is unable to produce any digital content, but is able to vary the *qualities* of its crying. They have different cries for different needs, which is how mothers can appear almost psychic to others in terms of knowing if her baby is hungry, wet, frightened etc.

When listening to music, the left hemisphere processes the words and meaning, while the right hemisphere hears the tune. When most people hear a song, they are able to appreciate both the words and the tune, and they don't hear them separately, as long as the two hemispheres are integrated. However, with sufficient damage to the right hemisphere, people often become completely tone deaf. Meanwhile, damage to the left hemisphere often wipes out the ability to process the words, but the tune can still be appreciated.

The two hemispheres communicate with each other via a structure called the corpus callosum. Some time back, neurologists had a propensity for severing this band of nerve fibres in order to treat some serious and otherwise untreatable types of epilepsy, because it had the effect of confining a seizure to the hemisphere where it began. This was a pretty bold move, considering that the corpus callosum contains more than 300,000,000 fibres that connect every part of one hemisphere to its corresponding part in the opposite hemisphere.

This operation, a "commissurotomy," produced some pretty interesting results, depending on your point of view. Devoid of direct communication with each other, in some patients a strange type of competition between the two brains emerged. One lady was reported to have great difficulty in getting dressed in the morning, because each hand would reach for a different dress.

Neurologist V.S. Ramachandran reports a curious example of a 59-year-old woman who had suffered damage to her corpus callosum:

> . . . she had one extraordinary complaint—every now and then her left hand would fly up to her throat and try to strangle her. She often had to use her right hand to wrestle the left hand under control, pushing it down to her side— much like Peter Sellers portraying Dr. Strangelove. She

sometimes even had to sit on the murderous hand, so intent was it on trying to end her life. (36)

This same kind of division often occurs without the benefit of a commissurotomy, when different aspects of someone's experience are not well integrated.

A client arrives in your office and says, "I do try *not* to worry, Doctor—you see, I *tell* myself that I should be happy and grateful, but I cannot help but get this awful *feeling* of resentment." Ask yourself which hemisphere is expressing which part?

There are other examples such as, "I'm of two minds about it. On one hand I really feel like I want to go, but on the other I ask myself if this is really a good idea" and, "I hear you telling me that everything is fine, but I still get this uneasy feeling."

We can begin to hear how the hemispheric divide is often expressed in everyday life, indicating which aspects of someone's experience need more integration. The key to this kind of division is often the word "but" and one ridiculously easy way to begin to heal the division is to use the word "and" instead.

"Doctor—you see, I tell myself that I should be happy and grateful, *and* I cannot help but get this awful feeling of resentment."

Hearing Voices

"If you hear voices, it's best you don't tell your psychiatrist.
He won't understand, and will just think you are crazy."
—Clive, dispensing psychiatric advise.

The phenomenon most commonly associated with schizophrenia is hearing voices. However, in my experience hearing voices isn't half as common in schizophrenics as might be believed, and it is also far more common in the general population than usually realized. Only two types of people don't hear voices—dead people and psychiatrists, and the latter are undoubtedly kidding themselves. Dead people don't hear voices because, well, they are dead. Psychiatrists cannot hear voices because they are too well-educated into believing that any report of internal auditory experience requires immediate diagnosis and observation.

It is ironic that a psychiatrist can look at a schizophrenic and say to himself (internal voice), "That man is hearing voices; he must be psychotic." It worries me even more that psychiatrists (and other people for that matter) say things to themselves that they apparently don't hear! The guy may be crazy, but "hearing voices" is not a good basis for a "differential diagnosis."

We *all* hear voices. Have you ever had an argument with your boss in your head? Ever had that annoying song stuck in your head all day? Ever felt bad as you replayed that criticism you received for something you did—or did not do—so long ago? These are all examples of hearing internal voices—you might call it "daydreaming," "thinking," "imagining" or whatever. But strangely, if you are diagnosed as "schizophrenic" then we'd call the *same* internal activity "voice hearing" or "hallucination."

Somebody asked me once what I thought deaf schizophrenics would hallucinate. My guess is that they hallucinate *communication* just like everyone else. Brain-scan studies of voice hearers have demonstrated repeatedly that the same part of the brain is active in both "voice hearing" and normal internal dialogue. Functionally speaking, there is no difference between them—it's a matter of intensity, context, semantics, degree of certainty, and our ability to ignore, or not hear them.

It's important to know where your client's internal voice appears to be located. "Inside my head" is the most common answer, and of course that's quite accurate; that's where it is. The next most common response is for someone to gesture near their ear—usually the left one—indicating that it is outside the head, usually nearby.

One interesting phenomenon reported by schizophrenics is that of external voice hearing, in which the voice is experienced as originating at some distance from the person. The voice comes from the fireplace, or from another room. Many non-schizophrenics experience something like this on the cusp of sleep when they may hear someone calling their name. Typically these experiences are very short in duration, maybe just a single syllable, whereas a schizophrenic's external voices might persist for hours—again a matter of degree.

When an internal voice is a problem, the emotional tone is never one of pure love and light. When your client arrives wearing earplugs or a tinfoil helmet, this might give you a little clue as to what they are experiencing. If he is wearing earplugs *and* a tinfoil helmet then you are definitely in for an interesting afternoon.

When you *only* hear a voice, many of the meaningful details of the communication are lost, just as when you talk with someone on the telephone—the context, the facial expression and posture of the person talking, what they are doing, etc., is not available to you. Nearly all mental experience overlaps into all modalities. With voice hearing we might just need to uncover, or bring these other modalities into conscious awareness in order to gain access to the portion of experience that will be useful. Expanding someone's experience of a voice to include these details requires recovering the visual modality.

"OK, so as you hear that voice now, if that voice were a person and that person were in this room now, point to where that person is."

The client points, and says, "Over there."

"OK, now which way is that person facing?"

"Facing me."

"And how far away are they?"

"About three feet, really close."

"And what expression do they have on their face?"

This kind of question elicits the visual representation of the voice, and now there are a million and one things you can do. It is generally best that you choose what to do according to the client in front of you, and not according to what you read in a book. But as a guideline here are some useful principles:

If you increase the distance between the client and the visual representation, that will proportionally reduce the volume of the voice, because things that get further away tend to get quieter.

Changing the location of an image in this way is an example of an *analogue* change, one that can vary over a wide range. Most people try to eliminate an unpleasant voice completely. Not only is that very difficult; it results in losing any useful information that the voice might have to offer. Making an analogue change is much easier than complete elimination, and when the voice is quieter, it is easier to listen to it and find out if it might be trying to communicate something useful.

When someone slides an image all the way away from them, it is important to know *where* it is going to end up. They might slide it in front of them, or behind them, or off to the side, or wherever. If they slide it into their future timeline into the slot of "four weeks away," then the chances are pretty good that they'll have their problem back again in four weeks' time. You also risk creating a situation in which they will avoid their future.

Sometimes I deliberately slide a representation into next week so that it will come back. With some clients this can be an important maneuver, because with some clients it is only with this kind of experience that they will begin to take charge of their own neurology. Rather than "spoon feeding" the answers to them, I encourage clients to explore their own representational systems and start observing what changes they can initiate. Too many "difficult" clients want to be given the answers, or told what to do, only to admit later that they didn't actually try any of it for themselves, but they did "think about it."

Occasionally they don't get it, and need to be advised to slide a troubling image behind them. Or you could ask them to slide it all the way away from them until it drops over the horizon. I want a client to be able to do this kind of simple exercise for themselves, and I assure them that I'll be checking up to make sure that they do.

I'm unlikely to "cure" a schizophrenic overnight with this kind of exercise, but I *can* begin to give him more control over his life and thinking processes. It's much like eating an elephant—take one bite at a time. An occasional kick in the pants is sometimes helpful, too.

This kind of analogue change is seldom permanent and lasting *unless* you do something else to lock it into place. For instance, "dropping the image over the horizon" introduces a *digital* change that may keep the image from sliding back on its own. Once an image is "over the horizon," it is gone—*completely* gone—in contrast to just farther away and smaller.

I want people to begin to take control of their mental machinery, so that they can change how they think about their thinking. To deliberately go inside and apply conscious thought to create a change seems to be a very rare event on this planet. For so many people (schizophrenic or not) thinking is rather like sitting in front of the television set—often disliking the current program but lacking the ability to get up and change the channel.

Once you have elicited the visual representation of a voice, here's another approach you can take. Back in the glorious 1980's when psychedelic children's TV programs were at their height, one program featured a curiously annoying cartoon character known as Zippy. Zippy had the misfortune of having a zipper for a mouth and when he talked too much, the colourful and campy presenter zipped him up—possibly inadvertently affecting the sexual development of thousands of precocious young viewers.

When changing the content of a representation there tends to be a congruence across modalities. Thus a zip on the mouth of the person in the visual image produces the expected corresponding change in the auditory portion of the experience. Simply put—no mouth; no talking—another digital change.

For one disturbed lady, putting a zip on the mouth of one of her hallucinatory voices just made it angrier, and as a result she became increasingly disturbed. Her day-to-day activity seemed to consist of little more than spending all day trying to appease an angry part of herself. In this situation we did Connirae Andreas' Core Transformation process (3) on this part and produced one of the most dramatic transformations in a client I have ever witnessed.

Many of my schizophrenic clients have somehow managed to personify their voices into independent entities with a life of their own. In a videotaped session of Richard Bandler working with a schizophrenic, Andy reports that he is being persecuted by Mary, a character in the TV series, "Little House on The Prairie," something surely horrible enough to give just about *anyone* nightmares!

Bandler used a similar "Bugs Bunny Cure," with Andy, named after the classic cartoon episode where Bugs and the artist are locked into a recursive relationship. The artist tires of Bugs complaining and erases his mouth. Bandler got Andy to use a mental eraser to rub out the mouth from the image of Mary from the Prairie. Such a technique often works well; give it a try on some of your own internal representations that you wish were quieter, especially those critical voices that belong to other people. However, it does require eliciting a visual image of who is speaking.

As mentioned earlier, when you make a representation bigger or closer, the auditory volume will typically increase proportionally. However, increasing the auditory volume is not going to necessarily produce an increase in the size of the visual component. For example, I can shout louder without having to make myself bigger or come closer to you.

People have brought me their gargoyles, biblical figures, mythical talking creatures, archangels, devils, and creatures I just could not recognise or even begin to understand. One memorable client regularly found himself holding court with the Devil and Jesus, who would be arguing about the moral issues pertinent to his life. I initially proposed putting zips across their mouths and then padlocking them shut, but my client told me that to do such a thing would be sacrilegious.

One client had a little imp sitting on his left shoulder that chattered all day long, while another had a small novelist that sat on his shoulder describing his every action from an observer position in the style of a '50s crime novel. It's worth paying close attention to these things. Keep your head still and take a look at your *left* shoulder and as you do so, remember the eye accessing cues chart.

Remembered auditory voices tend to be accessed down to the left, where the imp and the novelist were. The modalities of "hallucinations" and their submodalities are of vital importance here. Throw away that DSM IVR (18), the definitive shopping list for mental maladies, the Bible of psychiatrists everywhere—and start paying attention to your clients instead. If you are attending to an internal voice, that makes it hard to hear what is happening outside. Your clients have probably been telling you far more that you ever heard.

A method that simply will *NOT* work is that of getting the client to argue back to his voices. This is a serious error that just sets up a combative relationship—something I have observed far too many times in psychiatric facilities. This starts an especially tiring escalation, and before long you may find the patient over in the city centre shouting at passing cars. On the other hand, negotiating for peace with voices may sometimes be of benefit.

Two typical and particularly unhelpful suggestions that I've heard from psychiatric staff are, "Just ignore them" or "Just tell them to be quiet." Having said that, in one monotonous institution that was pervaded by a sense of helplessness and hopelessness, I introduced my particular brand of therapeutic anarchy. Once I ran bursting into an agitated patient's room shouting, "*Please* tell those God-damned voices of yours to shut the hell up, they are driving *me* crazy!" and then stormed back out of the room. I guess this changed the dynamic of the relationship between him and his voices. Thus suitably chastised, and with the combative relationship with the voices shifted onto me, he changed state. He found me later and apologized, and thereafter continued to demonstrate signs of improvement.

Along with glitter trails, I like to add at least a little enjoyable disorder and chaos into otherwise dull and static environments. I taught NLP to some of the patients and did my drug round by shouting, "Right you lot, time to get drugged up! Come and get 'em! We've got pink ones, blue ones and rainbow-flavoured ones that are all assured to keep you all under control for the afternoon!"

These patients soon started to protest to me that they weren't really as crazy as I was making out. In fact some even went as far as suggesting that *I* was the crazy one and was in need of "special coffee"—meaning that they'd lace it with thorazine.

What is interesting about this apparently anarchic and irresponsible approach is that these patients responded by taking *more* responsibility. On "socialisation" visits out of the unit and into town, patients who were previously "psychiatrically disinhibited" would sometimes express concern that I wouldn't do anything to embarrass them.

Normally, at the end of each shift, the staff would normally write up a report on each patient. I found this odd, because most of the time the staff appeared to spend much of their working day in the staff room, smoking with the door closed. It always seemed wrong to me that it was the staff evaluating the patient's performance and not vice-versa. So I removed the door to the staff room and I got the patients to start writing daily performance reviews on the staff. But I found that this isn't the ideal way of retaining paid employment.

Changing Position

One technique I use a lot that has produced some results that are as dramatic as the Core Transformation process came from something a psychotherapist told me that sounds much like something Virginia Satir (4) might have done—maybe I read it in one of her books. In doing family therapy, she had a family where the impasse was between the father and his 17-year-old son. The father was a "strong" and stoical man, for whom expressing emotion was not an easy or desirable skill. She had the son go and stand behind the seated father and gently place a hand on each of his father's shoulders in order to "feel and relieve some of the tension there." Apparently this was of great effect in changing the relationship between father and son, so naturally it got me thinking.

As I have mentioned previously, the internal representations of problem people are rarely, if ever, radiating beauty and light. I'll often ask what the expression on their face is, and what their posture is. Then I'll ask the client to imagine walking behind that person and gently placing a hand on each shoulder and giving just a little gentle massage to loosen the person up a bit. As the client imagines touching the person, this also shifts the kinesthetic submodalities. Usually the representation itself changes, relaxes, or even starts crying. For instance:

Client: "I feel criticised."

Therapist: "What has to happen inside for you to feel criticised?" (Since criticism is a largely verbal activity. I could have asked, "And who criticizes you, and what do they say?")

C: "I hear a voice."

T: "And if that voice were a person, who would that be?'

C: "My father. My father was always criticising me; he had a horrible voice like that." (Client has not seen father for over 14 years.)

T: "And if your father were in the room now, where would he be?"

C: "Standing right in front of me, really close."

T: "That's right. Now close your eyes. I want you to imagine walking around behind him and gently place one hand on each of his shoulders and whisper into one ear that is close enough to hear you, to 'Relax now. . . all the way.' . . . (pause) . . . Tell him it's OK . . . it's OK . . . and gently massage those shoulders; give him a moment to relax, all the way down now. . . ."

Try this now yourself; think of someone you felt inferior to as a child, and hold that representation in mind. Then stand up, go around behind them, and gently massage their shoulders and notice the difference. . . .

This is a nice maneuver that achieves several things simultaneously. Primarily it completely shifts the spatial orientation of the client in relation to the representation. Instead of facing each other in opposition, they become oriented in the same direction, with implications of alliance and cooperation. In addition, massaging someone's shoulders and talking to them in this way presupposes a much more friendly relationship than criticism does, opening the door to a more understanding attitude.

One aspect of this is worth pointing out, as it isn't always obvious at first. When you elicit a representation from a sitting client and then ask them to stand up, the representation tends to stay where it is in geographical space. A representation that is a negative artefact from childhood is often bigger, or higher up than the client, and because of this it often represents something more powerful than the client. However, when you stand up and massage someone's shoulders, you are the same height, with implications of equality. And when you feel equal to someone else, you feel much less defensive and protective.

In my early daze, I would try to get the client to reduce the size of the representation, or "push" it further away. Invariably they would find some kind of difficulty. Then I chanced upon the move described above, which is much more graceful and effective.

Essentially, this puts the client in control of the representation, and gets the representation to relax. The representation is exactly that—a representation of a part of himself, a bit of his own psyche that isn't feeling nice. This is a hugely powerful technique. I prefer to have the client remain sitting and do this in their imagination. However, it isn't unusual for someone to actually stand up and go through the physical motions of these activities.

Are NLPers Scared of Schizophrenia?

"When making the helmet, it is vital that you put the shiniest side of the foil outermost." —Advice from Heroic Howard when discussing ways to avoid "thought insertion" from the planet Uranus.

While working in an acute psychiatric facility, I asked the staff to show me their most unstable schizophrenic. I was introduced to a curious lady (who, despite her forcible detention within the facility, was euphemistically referred to as a "resident"—without even a hint of irony). Despite all the drugs, electroshock, detention in the rubber seclusion room and attempts at reasoning, there had not been one single positive change in the woman's behaviour, yet the staff thought of her as "unstable." Even after 3 months of such treatment she still remained under 24/7 "eyeball" supervision. She clearly hadn't improved one little bit, and in a game without end, her negative behaviours increased proportionally to the attempts by the staff to get her to quiet down.

What was most impressive was that the staff had needed to remove all electrical sockets because she had developed a new "symptom" of grabbing hold of a nurse and running towards anything electrical in order to insert something, *anything*, into the live wires. She clearly didn't intend to be taken down alone.

She was a powerfully-built woman who wouldn't communicate verbally with anyone but she would happily communicate kinaesthetically. For the staff she became a logistical nightmare, as they now had to eat with plastic cutlery and remove all the foil from everyone's cigarette packets.

There was also the problem of the light bulbs and sockets. So understandably they had a strong interest in trying to understand exactly why she did that, and how she could be stopped without keeping her locked up in the rubber room 24 hours a day.

Well, I immediately wondered if it had anything to do with the fact that she was being forcibly electroshocked under a Mental Health Section, so I gave her a pair of rubber boots. (I was already wearing mine.) "Thanks" she said, "Now I can take out *every single one of those fuckers* before they finally get me." Sometimes it's just a question of paying attention to the right detail to get the right kind of response.

Despite the remarkable stability of this woman's behavior in the face of all the ECT and industrial strength madication she had been given, none of the staff had recognised any patterns in her behaviour. They all operated within their ruling belief system that since she was diagnosed with "hebephrenic schizophrenia" eventually the drugs would correct her "chemical imbalance" and she would "calm down." Despite the evidence right there in front of them that this was not working, the drugs were still being forcibly given several times a day.

"She seems pretty angry," I suggested.

"Yes" the chief nurse said, "that is her *biggest* problem."

Her biggest problem?

In "Wisdom, Madness and Folly" (28) R.D. Laing wrote of a ward where he ordered the doors to be unlocked and the drugs thrown away. Sure, at first windows got broken and chairs thrown about. But things soon calmed down—after all, how do you rebel when there is nothing to rebel against?

Once we can see through the nominalizations of psychiatric psychobabble we can begin to design interventions for the specific individual rather than relying on the carpet-bombing approach of mass madication. Just as there is a tendency for psychiatric professionals to lean towards "reality orientation," there is a tendency in NLP to challenge nominalizations or meta-model violations. Neither of these approaches will be much help in working with schizophrenia; they will only create distance between NLPer and patient—as well as between NLPer and psychiatric professional!—something I have learned to my own cost and marginalisation by the psychiatric industry.

I have tried arguing against beliefs before—everything from a conviction in God through to a paranoid who thought he *was* God. It's exhausting work, and while it is possible to win by attrition, usually they'll only "change their minds" in order to get rid of me.

Effective therapists don't challenge schizophrenic realities, but rather *join* them and *expand* them. After all, a universal feature of a schizophrenic's world is its rigidity, poverty, and tightness, and most of all, its sheer stability in the face of logic, reason, and extreme patience.

While many writers have commented on the metaphorical nature of schizophrenic communication, one NLP approach is to take the communication at its literal face value. As Richard Bandler suggests, if schizophrenics are not in touch with reality, we can change reality so that they *are*.

For example, Bandler saw a patient who heard voices coming out of the wall plugs. He put speakers in the wall plugs, and then talked to the patient using the speakers, giving him some *real* voices from the wall plugs to compare to the voices that he already heard. That offered the patient an opportunity to distinguish between the voices in his head and the ones actually coming from the speakers.

For the paranoid who believes that he is being followed everywhere, having him actually followed everywhere (thus making his delusion real) creates a situation in which he can sort out whether an experience is real or simply a delusion. However, I have found this too difficult a concept for the consideration or comprehension of disciplinary panels with whom I have been involved.

Dr. Al Siebert tells us in his article about non-diagnostic listening (43) of a girl who heard the voices of God. Siebert asked, "Why is it that of all women in the world, God chose you to be the mother of the second Saviour?" He didn't ask this as a challenge, but rather to open up her world a little bit.

Bandler also tells of the schizophrenic who claimed to be Jesus Christ. Bandler neither challenged this delusion (which invariably results in failure) nor sought the reason why he might escape his reality in this way. Bandler's approach was simply to take the man at his word and to bring with him a large cross and a hammer and some nails. Only Bandler himself can tell us if he really *would* have hammered the nails all the way through, but I am sure that the patient himself had no doubt about it, because he immediately began to protest that he wasn't really Christ.

According to Jay Haley (25) all communication occurs at the following four levels:

Communicator
> *Message*
>> *Recipient*
>>> *Context*

Or, more simply:
I (*communicator*)
> am saying something (*message*)
>> to you (*the recipient*)
>>> here and now. (*context*)

A schizophrenic is unable to communicate on two or more of these levels, or actively seeks to negate them. For instance, on introduction to a chronic schizophrenic lady who was twice my age, her opening line to me was, "Are you my father?" Thus she is negating herself as the *communicator* (i.e. she is not who her communication purports her to be), she is negating me the *recipient* (clearly I am not the person that her communication suggests) and she negates the *context* (I am a member of staff being introduced to a patient, not a father being reunited with his daughter.) And all these negations also negate the *message* as a whole.

Of course the flip side of all this is that she is behaving *perfectly* according to the context—we expect "patients" in the madhouse to say weird things that make little apparent sense.

From the case notes, I knew that she greeted everyone this way. And when a staff member denied being a relation she would respond viciously with, "Don't *lie*! Why are you *always* lying?" and thus began the usual psychotic exchange.

When she says, "Hello, are you my father?" despite the fact that she was twice my age and her father was a long time dead, what I need to do is to reconnect her negated levels back to her, the speaker.

So quite naturally my response was simple; I told her that yes, I *was* her father, so now where is my kiss? As I puckered up she laughed and told me not to tell such lies, but seeing as I was such a fine-looking young man (not her father) she'd still like to steal a quick kiss anyway. I promptly fled doing my very best Daffy Duck impression and hid in the kitchen. This meant that she was cued to come to me, rather than the usual setup of the staff continuously going to her. This exchange re-wrote the rules of engagement with which she was familiar, and thus change had begun.

Note that she didn't ask, "Am I your daughter?" This would have been an entirely different paradigm. It was not her *own* identity that she was establishing but that of the other people around her. The negation of her own identity is established by implication of the question. If she had asked me, "Am I your daughter?" in similar circumstances I would have replied something along the lines of, "Yes! Where on earth have you been?"

In "Tell Me I'm Here," (17) Anne Deveson gives an example of a simple exchange between herself and her schizophrenic son.

"Who's responsible for me, Anne?"

"You are."

"I am? I'm sorry I hassle you, Anne."

Note that Anne is his mother but the questioning is not to her, it is to *Anne*. Her son is implying that someone is responsible for him, i.e. his mother, but he is not addressing his mother in those terms but rather as an equal.

The trend is for this type of schizophrenic to continually call the other person's identity into question. I have often witnessed interactions between staff and patient that revolve around the staff member reassuring the patient regarding the staff member's identity. This is especially true when new members of staff arrive on the unit. I have heard schizophrenics challenge the identity of the new guy with utterances such as, "Are you from the CIA?" "Have you come to take me away to prison?" or my favorite, "You are Satan!" bellowed at me unexpectedly by a female patient who immediately attempted to bite my genitals. Of course this succeeded in eliciting a rapid and significantly defensive maneuver.

By controlling the apparent identity of those with whom they communicate, the schizophrenics invariably succeed in controlling the direction of the conversation, with the staff continually on the "back foot" defending their own identities. Essentially, the relationship that is being established by the schizophrenic is, "I won't let you be you; you will only be who I permit you to be."

One client used to tell everyone, "I haven't got a head." They took her literally and reassured her that she did indeed have a head, but she didn't believe them. So in order to help her, they diagnosed her as psychotically depressed and gave her electroshock. I'm not entirely sure how this was supposed to help, but after about 90 shocks she still didn't have a head, so they drugged her with industrial strength neuroleptics instead. She continued to say, "I haven't got a head" despite incremental dosage increases and repeated blood tests.

To explain what happened next I shall need to borrow a joke from Abraham Maslow, about a man who thought he was dead. The doctor asked the patient, "Do corpses bleed?" "Of course not," says the patient. The doctor first asks permission to test this, and then sticks a pin in the patient and squeezes out a drop of blood. "I'll be damned!" exclaims the man—"Corpses *do* bleed, don't they!"

The staff tried getting clever, "How can you eat then?" they'd ask her. She'd point to her neck and shoulders and say, "Feel that, that is food, see, that is food!" Great! Not only did she still not have a head, but she now also had food in her shoulders. The next step occurred with the inevitable, "How do you talk then if you haven't got a head?" Well, now she had direct thought transmission. Next came, "Why do you brush your hair, then?" So she stopped washing and brushing her hair, which is a change of sorts, I guess. And on and on it went. I wondered just what else the staff could come up with to install inside this poor woman.

What the staff failed to see was that the head was right there on top of her neck all along. Maybe if the staff hit her hard enough with that hardback copy of the DSM-IVR diagnostic manual (18) they could have anticipated a slight change in direction. After all, what could she say, "You bastards! Don't hit my head!"? We should certainly hope so.

I'm reminded of Milton Erickson's patient who wouldn't eat because he didn't have a stomach and was being tube fed. Erickson put a lot of baking soda in his next "meal," and the resulting bout of belching as the soda reacted with stomach acid gave powerful notice that he certainly did have a stomach after all.

There are other patterns at work here.

Let's compare the following communications:

"I have heart burn"

"I haven't got a head."

While neither statement is literally true, both conform (partially at least) to cultural norms. "Heartburn" relates well to the sensation that occurs with acidic gastric reflux, and more than one person has "lost their head" in a crisis. So what might you say to a patient who thinks that she hasn't got a head? Well, sometimes people "lose their minds" and you just need to know where to look for it. Many metaphorical statements about experience are required by culture. If I were to tell you that I was suffering from "heartburn" throwing a bucket of water at my chest will help far less than an antacid.

Across different cultures metaphorical descriptions of the same event will vary enormously, and that is why identifying a mental illness in a totally foreign or alien culture would be an insurmountable task. As Haley pointed out, much of schizophrenic communication is an attempt at *not* communicating, which is itself a paradoxical double bind. How can you communicate that you are not communicating? The schizophrenic concerned was indeed having quite a slow burning and serious life crisis, having been incarcerated and madicated for over 18 years.

According to Haley's model, "I have heartburn" is a positive statement that does not negate on any level (depending on context). It is a positive and true statement that does not negate the identity of the speaker, the communication itself is readily understood by any listener who speaks English as their native language, and the communication does not negate the listener's identity. Meanwhile, the context is appropriate where the speaker is making the statement within a relationship whereby the listener is able to offer a response (verbal or nonverbal) congruent with the communication.

However, "I haven't got a head" negates on a fourfold level and is a communication based on a non-communication. I was working as residential worker within a psychiatric facility in which this woman was "voluntarily" detained. "I haven't got a head" was her response to me introducing myself to her. She promptly fell to the floor clutching her throat, making choking noises and kicking her legs. I was a bit taken aback, but I was assured that this was "normal" behaviour for her on meeting someone new.

There are many possible responses to someone without a head. We could try to de-nominalise with, "Where is it then?" or "How did you come to lose it?" or simply, "Well, that was bloody careless!" but we need to consider just which direction we want to go with it. There are very few schizophrenic behaviours that frighten me. So to be introduced to a female "resident" without a head who was pretending to choke, I stayed within the context of our meeting and immediately started fussing about the possible mess she might make on the carpets.

I am reminded of one client who told me he was "dead." My reflex response was, "Shit! How did that happen?" and I listened patiently for about 45 minutes while he told me all about it. "Sounds like an awful thing to happen to a guy," I told him as I went to make a cup of tea. Curiously, from that day he never once claimed to be a corpse again. Of course, the psychiatric staff wrote in the notes, "Patient finally appears to be responding to Respiridone."

More than one observer of residential psychiatric practice has commented that most of the staff seem to "walk on eggshells" with their patients, lest they trigger a psychotic episode or symptom. Far too many patients run their wards by the "potential tyranny of psychosis"—the fear of what psychotic trick the patient will pull next.

There is an old joke about the new gorilla being introduced to the other experimental test subjects in the lab. The older gorilla shakes his hand and says, "Hey dude, if you press that lever you can get that man over there to give you a banana." All too often, it is the staff that are being trained by their patients, rather than vice-versa; and the patients are generally a *lot* better at it.

In psychiatry there is a big emphasis on patients being "stabilised" and thus humour and joviality are frowned on. Humour is somehow equated with being "unprofessional" or "stupid." However, humour always involves looking at something differently, a skill that most patients (and most staff!) desperately need, and it creates a relationship based on something *different* from what the patients are familiar with.

This approach contradicts much of what the psychological fields promote with their emphasis on the "therapeutic relationship." That firmly establishes a "therapist-patient" context and it is from within that rather small and stable context that the therapist attempts to *stop* the patient from *being* a patient. Does this not seem a bit strange to you, too? This unrecognised and unacknowledged double bind really needs to be tackled well before the person acting as "therapist" can ever hope to create any profound and lasting change in his client.

It's worth mentioning at this point some differences in the structure of a psychotic reality. In the examples above, all the clients were *globally* affected. Their entire reality and day-to-day experience was built upon a very stable and enduring set of beliefs. Thus with the guy who believes himself to be Jesus, nailing him to the cross might break the globalised effect and reconnect him to the outside world, but it isn't necessarily going to enable him to organise his thoughts or life any differently. This is especially true when he resides within the trappings of a psychiatric "care" facility.

This is a totally different state of affairs from the *partially* affected psychotic whose delusion happily co-exists with an otherwise normal life. Thus someone may have a strong religious conviction—whether it is the common concept of God, or an extra-terrestrial deity from the planet Zog—but still manage to interact within our communities in acceptable ways.

The number of people who share the same belief might simply determine the level of delusion in this category. If you are on your own, they are going to drug you—but if you get yourself a following, you might be declared a minister and even become a respected pillar of the community. To what extent the above applies to psychiatrists and psychologists, I will let you, the reader, determine.

When I represented a private patient of mine at a mental health tribunal hearing, I asked the panel to do two things for me:

1. I asked them to convince me of their ability to treat him, because despite over 100 hospital admissions, the patient was clearly no better today than when they started with him more than 8 years earlier. So it seemed reasonable to me that if they were going to detain him for another year, then they should surely be able to prove their ability to treat him effectively. As far as I could tell their performance was seriously lacking any credibility since the psychiatrist told me that the patient had shown the "predictable level of deterioration" over time. (Nice one—blame the patient for your own incompetence.)

2. I wanted one person present on the panel to prove to the rest of the room that they were themselves sane. I needed this so that my client would have a model of sanity to follow, and know what he had to do to be set free. Every person in that room declined my request, and yet they continued to demand that my client himself prove his sanity!

David Rosenhan is a psychologist famous for his 1972 experiment that was written up in an article titled, "On Being Sane in Insane Places." (40) He had eight graduate students admit themselves to psychiatric hospitals with vague complaints. Once admitted, they did nothing out of the ordinary and behaved normally. Curiously, the other patients recognized that they were sane, but the staff didn't! These graduate students had great difficulty getting discharged, because their requests were categorized as further evidence of their insanity. Eventually they were let go, but none of them were discharged "sane"; they were all discharged with "schizophrenia in remission." Once you have crossed the threshold into psychiatric care and become labeled, getting free again or remaining unmadicated can be extremely difficult.

When dealing with schizophrenia, the NLPer faces challenges both on the inside and on the outside of the patient's reality. There is not only the internal disorganization, but the rigid psychiatric context to deal with. I think this complication, and the involvement with the psychiatric services that is often necessary is what puts so many NLPers off working with psychiatric clients. I was recently surprised to learn that one well-known NLP trainer to whom I referred a young man with an obsessive-compulsive disorder immediately referred him on to a psychiatrist for an evaluation. The trainer's concern was that the young man might be suffering from "schizophrenia" and thus might require medication and not "soft" psychological help. I called the psychiatrist, who stated that in his view the referral was totally unnecessary.

The young man returned to me with a small plasticine ball given to him by the NLP trainer. "I have to squeeze this when I feel stressed," he told me. "And how do you feel when you squeeze the ball?" I asked the young man. "Stressed" was the reply. We posted the ball back to its former owner.

Inevitably, the section of the population who are madicated daily and often not permitted to work have little hope of being able to afford the fees of even an average NLPer. I often wonder if this high fee level might be deliberate and with a hidden agenda. After all, it is much more pleasant to work with "YARVIS" clients— "Young, Attractive, Verbal, Intelligent, and Successful—the "worried well," instead of those poor unfortunates stuck in the trap of inherited poverty, inner city housing, crime and despair.

Although much research into schizophrenia is biologically based, geographical location (suburbia vs inner city) is a much better predictor. Biological research is cleaner, it's neater, it's more "politically correct." It's also a much, much more comfortable way for us who don't have to live that way to think about it—it doesn't challenge our model of living. As one therapist wrote to me, "Poverty is a maladaptive behaviour, and as such there is nothing wrong with punishing it." While poverty is not necessarily a discriminating feature in the occurrence of schizophrenia, it certainly profoundly influences its manifestation and prognosis. Only if you are wealthy can you or your family afford effective help (if you can find it!). The differences between the chronic wards of the state hospitals and private hospitals are enormous, and so are the attitudes of the staff.

A couple of years ago while attending an evening presentation at one of the London NLP groups, I watched with interest the behaviours of those attendees who were sitting close to a man with profound tardive dyskinesia (TD). TD is a nasty drug-induced disorder that produces facial grimaces, tics and other involuntary bodily movements. It is a chronic condition that is unacceptably common amongst people receiving psychiatric madication. Yet very few psychological professionals—let alone NLPers—have ever heard of it. After the break, despite being sat in the middle of a fairly tightly packed audience, there was a perceptible ring of empty seats all around where this man sat. I guess it is this distance that many people prefer to keep from those things that they don't really understand. A high consultation fee definitely helps maintain this distance, while creating an illusion of success.

We are increasingly moving our society toward control through psychotechnology—recent court cases have seen parents challenged for refusing to drug their children with behavioural modification drugs, and sometimes children are then taken into state sponsored care and drugged that way. Laws have been proposed (stopped, but currently under review) that will make it a crime for a patient released into the community to not take his medication. We have parents and schools increasingly viewing madication as a solution to their pains of urban living and the discipline problems created by our politically correct ideology. Rather than a taking a trip to Bedlam to see the lunatics, today a short trip into the city centre will more than suffice.

Take some fruit and a large flask of tea. Talk to the derelict people you meet right there on the park benches, and you will learn much.

Each day, people are forcibly given electric shocks to their brain—no judge, no jury, no independent witnesses, and most important of all, *no fuss*. People still have to live in tower blocks that smell of violence and urine. They might lack the economy and resources to escape, but their madications and thymoleptics are free.

My challenge to NLPers is to take a broader systems view of their potential client group, and apply the technology of NLP to the models of living both in the local and non-local systems and meta-levels. There is a common thread of anarchic thought that runs through the NLP community, ranging from simply reading Robert Anton Wilson (45) to an in-built distrust of the self-professed experts, but reading about it is simply not good enough. Surely we can do better than this?

Meeting Marian

"I'm a terrible lover. I've actually given a woman an anti-climax."
—Scott Roeben

Therapy is indeed a very strange concept; the ideas therapists are always coming up with continue to amaze me—and clients' willingness to go along with them amazes me even more. Hopi Ear Candles are an interesting pastime, and for the new age devotees there is always the mystical image of the Hopi Indians engaging in ancient healing rituals by sticking burning candles into each other's ears. But at the end of the day, no matter how mystical you get, it is always worth remembering to remove that candle before you begin to smell burning hair. My mother never actually told me not to put burning things into my ears, but somehow I just know if she had ever caught me doing it, I'd have been spanked for sure.

Colonic irrigation is another very popular one. At an alternative therapy centre where I once worked, the colonic irrigator had a 2-week waiting list for new appointments. It was very lucrative too, so I was told. With very little overhead (bucket, hoses, jug, pump and a roll of tissue) you can flush colons and release all those nasty toxins at a neat £65 per session. Since an average session is less than twenty minutes, that's £195 per hour with a full schedule—more than most lawyers get for doing much the same kind of work.

Shortly before I left the centre, the irrigator hit upon a better idea: he doubled his fees and advertised for "couples." The advertisement read, "This gentle detoxification program will cleanse your system of unwanted accumulated toxins and is perfect for couples seeking to create a purer sense of intimacy." I thought about this for a while and then quickly tried to put all those pictures out of my mind. Four weeks later, business was apparently so good that I was asked if I wanted to "train up" to work for him myself. "We are going to start advertising for bisexuals next week!" he told me excitedly. I put the telephone down, wishing I hadn't spent so many years developing my visualisation skills. Some things really are best imagined by someone other than myself.

And then there was Marian, a beautiful blonde "sexual therapist" from Denmark. At least, that was how she described herself when I got chatting with her during a break at a conference. With a degree in psycho-sexual counselling, master practitioner certificate in NLP, "accomplished" Reiki master and a registered counsellor, Marian had decided to embark on a slight twist to the traditional "talk all about it" approach—she actually fucked her clients to teach them how it should be done—Swedish style (whatever that means).

"You see, it is all about the *technique*, not the words," she told me emphatically. "So unless you get naked with these people, you will never find out what is really going on between them." If the guy suffered prematurity, she'd get between the sheets with the guy and teach him how to do things differently. If the problem were *between* the couple, she'd climb straight in there and tackle it. It was when she started to explain to me what she did when women complain of vaginismus ("A painful and often prolonged contraction of the vagina in response to the vulva or vagina being touched.") that I started feeling rather wobbly.

I was reminded of a conversation from several years ago. A friend of mine who was a physician working in the genito-urinary medicine department was asked to consult with a married couple who had been referred for a two-fold reason: 1. Failure to conceive, and 2. Persistent vaginismus.

"I just *knew* what was going on with them as soon as I saw them," she told me, "because I get this at least once a year." By way of explanation she said, "Let's say they are rarely the brightest kids on the block, and they retain a certain childhood misconception. If you are a child, were do babies come from?" she asked me.

"Mummy's tummy?" I venture.

"Right. And how do they get out of mummy's tummy?" she continued.

"Ahhh, . . . out through the belly button?"

"It comes as quite a shock when I tell them where they should be 'doing it' instead, I can tell you," she told me.

I asked her if she ever saw people whose problems were caused by penetration of "the wrong hole" (i.e. the tradesman's entrance) but I was assured that this was very rare, as apparently very rarely do children grow up with the misconception that babies come out of *there*.

But back to Marian. "They actually *let* you do this?" I asked her incredulously as I opened the window. "Yah, of course they do. That is what they pay me for," she answered ever so matter-of-factly.

So I guess there are clients for every type of therapist, no matter what kind of help they are offering. Marion charges £600 per session, *per person*. I asked if this was all-inclusive or if she had a menu of extras, you know, like a hand job £25, blow job £90? She huffed, clearly offended by my obvious and blatant ignorance. "You think I am just a common prostitute?" she protested, starting to look angry. Then she added—quite unnecessarily, I thought—"*You* probably think that anything more than two minutes of thrusting makes you a sexual athlete! For *you* I would charge *double*!" Sensing danger, I made some polite excuses and quickly made my exit.

It did occur to me that the high fee does help prevent the problems that could so easily arise. Just imagine Premature Peter saying to his wife, "Yes dear, it *is* helping, of course it is, . . . but I'm not quite ready yet. Let's give Marian a call and see if she'll come over again for some more 'therapy.'" (Nudge, nudge.)

Contingent Suggestions

From The Hypnosis Training Manual

The basic formula is that because "A" is happening, then "B" can or must happen also. "A" should be a something that is obviously true and "B" is your suggestion directing their attention.

While you _____ , you can _____ .
While you *sit in that chair*, you can *begin to relax.*
While you *take a deeper breath*, you can *go deeper.*

When you _____ , please _____ .
When you *close your eyes*, please *make yourself even more comfortable.*
When you *lift your left hand*, please *notice what is happening to the other hand.*

Don't _____ , until you really _____ .
Don't *go into trance*, until you really *try to stay fully awake.*
Don't *become aware of your blinking*, until you really *feel deeply relaxed now.*

You won't _____ , until _____ .
You won't *begin to open your eyes*, until *you are really ready to come fully back now.*
You won't *wake up from this beautiful trance state*, until *you become unconsciously aware of the emotional resources at your ready disposal.*

Why don't you _____ , as you begin to _____ .

Why don't you *really take the time to enjoy your time of relaxation* as you begin to *see new opportunities to feel good now.*

Why don't you *go even deeper inside* as you begin to *access those unconscious resources.*

The more you become _____ , the more you will _____ .

The more you become *aware of those good feelings stored inside*, the more you will *begin to live in a state of grace.*

The more you become *more deeply relaxed*, the more *endorphins can be sent to that part of your body that most needs them.*

As you begin to feel _____ , you can begin to unconsciously notice _____ .

As you begin to feel *that sensation build in your hand*, you can begin to unconsciously notice *the level of physical control of mind over body.*

As you begin to feel *that warm inner glow*, you can begin to unconsciously notice *how far out from your body it can spread.*

As you feel _____ , you can notice _____ .

As you feel *that certain sense of relaxation*, you can notice *a warmth building.*

As you feel *the comfortable weight of your body in the chair*, you can *notice how much more relaxed you can become.*

The feeling of _____ , will allow you to really begin to _____ .

The feeling of *relaxation* will allow you to really begin to *open up the energy centres now.*

The feeling of *energy* will allow you to really begin to *allow it to flow through your body.*

After _____ , then you can really begin to _____ .

After *opening your eyes*, then you can really begin to *see the world in a different and brighter way.*

After *reading this book*, then you can really begin to *find many more positive ways of feeling good in this world.*

No Talking In Class

"It is better to keep your mouth closed and let people think you are a fool than to open it and remove all doubt." —Mark Twain

Emily was five years old, happy, well-adjusted, from a good family. She had an elder brother with whom she played cooperatively, and her schoolwork was satisfactory. She was popular with her classmates and played and smiled a lot.

There was one slight problem though—since starting school, not a single word had passed her lips while she was in school. Not a single solitary sound. Not a laugh, not a cry, no syllable, nothing. She didn't even speak to the other children, even though she joined in all the games.

Something had happened in preschool. She went in happy one day, and came out unhappy. After that, not a sound. Her parents took her out of preschool and outside of school everything was normal. At home she was a perfectly normal child.

Later at primary school, the educational psychologist is called and does her stuff—but no effect—little Emily refused to speak. Lessons were structured, counselling offered. The play specialists became involved; they used dolls, role-play, games, anything—everything. But still no result. Nothing.

Reward systems were put in place, token economies instigated, stickers were issued, positive reinforcement implemented and praise was lauded. Everything was tried, but this young lady wouldn't utter a peep. *Still* nothing.

So I get called. "Austin, The Last Resort."

I arrive at the school only to find wee Emily was far cleverer than I could have imagined. She had trained every adult in the school to accommodate to her "problem." I start with retraining the teachers, getting them to notice the subtle ways that Emily was able to

99

metaphorically wrap them around her little finger. The staff were fantastic, and very dedicated, but despite our best efforts, still there was nothing. Rethink time.

Another day at school, I try working my magic on Emily directly. I have told the parents I am prepared to only do this once. I had no interest in embarking a child on a course of therapy for a problem that is likely to spontaneously resolve at some point in her future anyway.

For two hours, the little minx sat there not engaging me in any way. She didn't even appear to be refusing to engage. If a visible sign of refusal had arisen, the rest would have been easy. She did vomit over me once though, and I did begin to wonder if her head was going to spin 'round, but this wasn't the devil. This was just a little girl who, for reasons only known to herself, refused to speak at school.

I returned home without result—other than stinking of orange squash-flavoured vomit.

Three months later, I telephone the family to see if any progress had been made.

"Oh yes," the mother tells me happily, "Everything is fine now."

"Wow! What happened?" I ask, quite excited and curious.

"Oh, we just told her it was time to start talking in class and the teacher said the same."

"What happened when the teacher said that?'

"Oh, Emily just said, 'OK, Miss,' and she started talking straight away." Lesson learned: Always start with the obvious.

When I was 7, my mum lost her slippers and she couldn't find them anywhere. "Where's the last place you'd look?" my father asked. "The fridge," came the reply. "Start there," he said.

It's worth noting that my mum's missing slippers *were* indeed in the fridge. My parents puzzled over this for years afterwards. But what they never thought was that *I* knew where they were because *I* put them there. I don't know why I did it; I guess children just do strange things sometimes. At least *I* did.

The Right Man Syndrome (Narcissism)

"When men are most sure and arrogant they are commonly most mistaken, giving views to passion without that proper deliberation which alone can secure them from the grossest absurdities"
—David Hume

One particularly arrogant young man sought my services in order to improve his confidence in his presentation of himself to other people. A self-professed "expert" in verbal seduction techniques, he did not wish to change any aspect of *his* behaviour, since he believed that he already *knew* how to behave. What he actually wanted was to *feel* better about the responses that his self-important behaviours tended to elicit from other people. Other people quite sensibly tended to avoid him like the plague. I found a shocking example of this level of narcissism in Pendergrast's *Victims of Memory*.

> I've had a lot of therapy and read a lot of self-help books. I've learned to really love myself. I always pamper my inner child. I have overcome any tendency to feel guilt for anything I do. I'm real good at asserting myself and expressing my anger, and I don't let anyone abuse me in any way. I've worked particularly hard on my co-dependency. I've cut off all my dysfunctional relationships. I'm now ready for a perfect relationship but no one I meet matches my level of mental health. What can I do to get the love I deserve? (34, p. 490)

I am also reminded of a senior nursing colleague with whom I worked in a specialist treatment area. Her confidence was supreme, but as is usually the case with *supreme* confidence, her competency was seriously lacking. Until she was finally tackled on her poor performance, she had been blissfully unaware that for several years all her work had been continuously monitored and double-checked by her junior colleagues in order to prevent any serious incident. Her "confidence" deleted from her experience any possibility that she herself was responsible for many of the problems that arose on that unit, because, curiously, someone else was always to blame. After consulting in different areas of failing businesses, I have learned that this is not an entirely rare phenomenon.

These clients present an interesting problem to therapists. They arrive at the therapist's office demanding that the therapist help them, but simultaneously denying that there is anything in their own behaviour that needs changing. "There is nothing wrong with me, it is everyone else that is the problem. Help me deal with everyone else."

Since the only person who can be changed is the person in the room, this is an impossible situation, what is called an "ill-formed outcome" in NLP. In order to change those other people's responses, either they would have to come to a session, or the client would have to change what he (or she) is doing. If you can manage to point this out to them, that can sometimes be a beginning of reorienting them to the real problem. But even when it doesn't, it makes the situation clear, and avoids trying to do the impossible, though it may shorten the session, and your income considerably.

These people almost never show up actually looking for help: "I'm just too pompous, arrogant and insensitive to other's views and feelings, and I'd like to change that." But a spouse or child may drag them in because of the trouble and unhappiness they cause.

These narcissistic behaviours can be exasperating to even the most seasoned therapist, and of course narcissistic individuals are very adept in pointing out any failing they can identify in the therapist's behaviour, character, performance, etc. These clients are often very perceptive and talented in identifying another person's vulnerabilities and are quick to exploit these to render others *"less than"* when challenged, making it quite reasonable to dismiss what others say. One particular client, desperate not to be out-done, said to me aggressively, "You are too clever for your own good, and *that* will be your undoing."

I call this kind of client the "Right Man," a term I have borrowed from writer A. E. Van Vogt in his exploration of violent men. Most of us have probably met a Right Man in some context of our lives. They often tend to be successful, and often are bosses, managers, or senior colleagues, because they have succeeded in convincing others of their superior views and capabilities. Far too many clients of mine have them as a parent for me to think there isn't a correlation between Right Man syndrome and serious emotional disturbances in their offspring.

At home, the "Right Man" may alternate his mood with temper outbursts in order to get his own way, and sometimes a deep dive into depression when he doesn't get his way, and begins to suspect that his sense of self is a fragile charade. The depression is often an unwitting but effective manipulation and the family learns to be careful not to upset Dad.

The Right Man must always have his way and above all is afraid of losing face. "How dare you talk to me this way?" is a standard response to anything that might indicate a weak spot in his infallibility, something that he can never admit. The RM takes the blaming position of, "My anger/depression is a direct response to *your* behaviours, whilst your behaviours have nothing to do with me." People interacting with the Right Man often feel that their interaction is continually being controlled by him, and that their answers and responses are being manipulated to maintain his facade.

One curious feature is that the Right Man tends to particularly enjoy television shows that involve other people "getting caught." These patterns serve to shield The Right Man from the effects of his own behavioural patterns. He tends to negate feedback from other people in relation to his own behaviour. The relationship that he insists on is as follows: "I get to behave however I want to—*with impunity*—*you* are the one that has to make the adjustment and just accept *me* for what I am."

The effect upon others who have to deal with him is often exasperation, hopelessness, and helplessness. The Right Man often manages to leave a trail of anxiety, despair, self-doubt and depression everywhere he goes.

Pattern #1 "There Are No Shades of Grey" Black and White Thinking.

Moderation and mediation are not options, because communication is essentially one-way. Everything is either one thing or another; anything in between is simply not allowed. The Right Man will often be an alcoholic or will abstain completely. He either loves someone totally, or hates them emphatically. You are either completely on his side or you are against him totally, and so on. Yet oddly in spite of all the obvious behaviours to the contrary, he will often claim to not have a view on the matter at all.

Nearly everything in the Right Man's world is an extreme position and his communication with other people tends to force them to choose that position. Failure to conform to this way of thinking is usually interpreted—*and thus exploited*—as a weakness. This pattern is both a spontaneous thinking pattern *and* is often utilised effectively as a mechanism to control other people. For example, when asked to moderate his aggressive tone, one such Right Man replied aggressively, "Fine! Then I will stop speaking to you altogether." To which I simply replied, "Thank you."

Following a minor disagreement with a brother, one Right Man declared, "That man is never welcome in my house again. *Ever!*" Twenty years onward, his position still had not changed.

Pattern #2 "You Have Ruined Your Life" Catastrophisation and Permanency.

In the Right Man's world, nothing is transitional or temporary. Nothing is permitted to be a flow, a developmental stage, or process that people work through. In the Right Man's world everything becomes permanent.

In NLP terms, this is an extreme form of "overgeneralisation" where one incident is generalised across contexts to just about everything. A small event is blown out of all proportion to become a catastrophe. For example, one 8-year-old daughter of a Right Man did badly on her Monday morning spelling test at school. This was met with the declaration from the father that, "You will fail *everything* if you can't even pass a single bloody spelling test." Another scenario involved someone declaring that his adult son had "ruined his life" by getting a tattoo when he was 19.

Catastrophisation doesn't require a verbal depiction of the catastrophe—a "silent" catastrophic emotional reaction involving an extreme social withdrawal over a relatively minor event can be sufficient to send an unmistakable message when it is in the context of all the other Right Man patterns.

Pattern #3 "I Know You Better Than You Know Yourself" Superior Knowledge.

The Right Man *knows* the truth—i.e. the "real" character of a person, the character that the person manages to hide from everyone else, including themselves!

The Right Man knows better because he knows the "right" way his son *really* wanted to be living, that is, according to the rules and wishes of the father that were assumed to be the *desired* rules and wishes of the son.

Someone can actually be quite successful and happy, but if the Right Man has decided otherwise, he will always regard this person as an unhappy failure and there is nothing that person can do to change their position.

One Right Man, when describing the *real* character and personality of his son (aged 38 and quite successful) gave three examples of how his son was a complete failure. Two examples were from infancy, and the third "proof" was from an event that occurred on his son's 5th birthday party!

One of the popular games of The Right Man is to "*put people in their place*"—and of course this "place" is decided by The Right Man himself. He does this frequently should anyone attempt to "rise above their station" or to manoeuvre themselves around in the social hierarchy so well dominated by the Right Man.

Pattern #4 "I'm Only Doing *This* For *Your* Benefit" Selfless Duty.

This pattern occurs as a result of Pattern #3 ("Superior Knowledge") when the Right Man claims to be doing an action for the sake of another person. The action may be unnecessary or undesired, it may even annoy the person for whom the action is being done, but the recipient must display gratitude to avoid punishment for being "ungrateful."

One example that springs to mind is of a wife who was saving to buy herself a car—she wanted to have her own transport and independence. She wanted a second-hand station wagon so that she could take the children and friends out and about.

Just before she bought a car, she arrived home to find a brand new, small, bright green "city" car in the drive. Knowing of her intentions, the husband has bought it for her. It stood out, was smaller than she wanted and was more expensive than she and her husband could really afford. But of course the Right Man knew it was best for her, and he only bought it for *her* benefit.

The wife's choice was to reject the car and face the trauma of a full-blown Right-Man-in-indignation attack, or drive around conspicuously in a car that didn't suit her.

Pattern #5 "Just Desserts. Trapped By Your Own Words" Linguistic Wizardry.

The Right Man is adept at tracking another speaker's words and will look for the slightest ambiguity or contradiction and then exploit it. The Rule of Permanency is also invoked, so any contradiction expressed over time is also exploited. So something expressed last year that is contradicted today will be jumped upon quickly. Thus, the other speaker cannot have a change of mind, opinion, or desire where the Right Man is concerned—unless of course it agrees with the Right Man's views.

Pattern #6 "The End of The Matter" Finalisation.

This is easily identified in the Right Man by a number of catch phrases that exhibit the same characteristic: "I have the final word here and you and the subject at hand are therefore dismissed." Common catch phrases that shut down communication and ensure that the last word is maintained take the form of:

"Full stop!"
"Period!"
"And that is the end of the matter!"
"End of story!"
"There is no further discussion!"
"That's it!"
"I have spoken!"

These phrases are often accompanied with a fist banging down and/or a vertical or horizontal slicing motion with the palm of the hand downwards.

If challenged, the Right Man simply repeats the catch phrase with greater emphasis. If challenged further, an escalation will invariably lead to threats of violence or aggression.

Pattern #7 "I'm Warning You!" Indicators of Violent Threats.

The Right Man rarely gives violent threats, but will often to be seen giving an *indicator* of a violent threat. Rather than waving his fist in the face of another person whilst shouting, "Shut up or I will thump you!" he is more likely to use a dominant body posture and tonality, with a pointing finger. The whole nonverbal demeanor expresses, "I am dominant and will not be crossed by *you*."

Gregory Bateson gives a great analogy when referring to dogs at play and adult dogs cautioning pups: *"The playful nip denotes the bite, but it does not denote what would be denoted by the bite."* You might need to read that a few times before it makes sense. To paraphrase Bateson, "The pointing finger denotes a fist, but does not denote that which is denoted by a fist."

This position enables the Right Man to deny ever being aggressive and enables him to experience other people's fear or submission as a weakness in them, rather than as feedback about his own behavior.

Pattern #8 Ask Loaded Questions, Deny Hidden Agenda. Be offended if Someone Asks Why You Are Asking.

For example, before the weekend, my client's father calls (A very rare event in itself, and usually a sign of something ominous.)

Father: "What are you doing over the weekend?"

Client (guarded, sensing trouble): "Not sure yet; why do you ask?"

Father: (demanding) "Well, what are your plans?" (Right Men lack spontaneity and assume everyone else must plan things meticulously too.)

Client: "I haven't decided yet; I have lots of things I might well do. So tell me, what are you thinking about?"

Father (defensively): "I just wanted to know if you had any plans?" (He pauses, cueing client to speak; he doesn't. Now offended/hurt) "I was going to take you out for dinner. My treat." (now as if crushed and hurting) "But if you are busy. . . ."

The important aspect of this is that the opening line of, "What are you doing over the weekend" isn't a neutral conversational piece as might happen in a chat between friends. It is a demand for information against which to measure a precise and as-yet-uncommunicated agenda.

The pattern is eliciting information about another's intention or activity without saying why. Curiously, one of this father's most common catch phrases is, "I have no hidden agendas." From what I observed, most people around him tend to be guarded when he starts asking for information, precisely because of the hidden agendas.

Attempts on the client's part to encourage the father to just communicate what he actually wants ("I'd like to take you to dinner on Saturday; my treat.") was met with the dismissive, "Stop psychoanalysing me." I'm told that he's much easier to be around as he's gotten older and taken retirement.

I've seen more exaggerated versions of this "hidden agenda" pattern in the parents of many emotionally disturbed people. The cruelest part is that when the "psychotic" is asked by mother, "What are you doing for the weekend?" and he freaks out, all anyone else sees is the poor mother asking a fairly normal question, so the freak-out appears to be a clear demonstration of the son's psychosis.

Pattern #9 Maintain One Level of Rapport, Whilst Violating Other Levels.

I experienced this a lot whilst working in the health service, with Right Man ward sisters who used the "management by mothering" strategy—molly-coddling people one second, and scolding them the next. The resulting uncertainty raises great anxiety amongst staff and leads to a highly bitchy environment with lots of infighting and bad gossip. Clients who arrive singing my praises and bearing gifts when I've never met them before, almost always turn nasty/hostile/argumentative before the session is over.

I think most Right Women become nurses and midwives. Some make it into education or business and turn into managers. Since moving offices at the college where I work two days a week, I have a ringside seat to a female Right Man Syndrome sufferer. This woman is a renowned bully, with a rather eccentric dress sense (I suspect colour blindness, or some brain abnormality) complete with 1950's Terse America, Librium Housewife hairstyle.

In my first encounter with her, she goes overboard with flattery in a way that says she is "buying" me, or as if she is exerting ownership over a possession. It's creepy. (Trojan Horse Strategy?) I politely and cautiously don't buy into her game, leaving her a little unsettled. I know there will be a penalty before long.

In our second encounter, she shouts at me inappropriately. Earlier in that day I had passed on a complaint brought to me by a group of students about a member of staff—trivial stuff, but something worth passing on to the management to resolve.

"The next time that you have a complaint about my department, I would appreciate it if you didn't go creeping off to Human Resources to tattle-tale," etc.

Of course, I am part of the human resources team, I tend not to "creep" anywhere, nor did I have any actual complaint myself about anything. I challenged her use of the words "creeping off"—something I am aware people don't often do with her—and she has stayed away from me since.

The pattern goes like this: Within the frame of being superior (i.e. in this case, a senior manager), holding that frame constant, break off all other rapport. So, whilst proclaiming herself to be a supportive, available, listening, and perfectly approachable manager, (She is none of those things.) she is simultaneously contradicting these statements in her behaviours and words. Her pattern is a clever one and I think I shall practice it myself to feed back to the (fortunately few in number) RM sufferers I know.

I am reminded of the literally dozens of scenarios I witnessed occurring in the health service where RM managers would systematically upset and undermine employees. Although in micro amounts each time, over long periods of time the employee would finally reach threshold and either resign, forward a grievance/complaint, or simply lose their temper and start having a go back. The level of reaction often appears massively disproportional to the thing the manager said at that moment. After all, it's the accumulation effect that is in play. So by way of explanation, the aggrieved party gives the history behind the situation, only to be told:

"If you have had a problem for all that time, why didn't you say something before?"—as though the complainant is utterly at fault for not having got upset sooner! But of course each little thing is itself insufficient to complain or take action over. Often when the person does complain, they can be dismissed as being too sensitive (after all, it was only a little thing).

Years ago I worked with one such exasperating manager, who fortunately tended to hide away in his office most of the time. He nearly always put his phone on "divert" so that for reasons never explained, I ended up getting all his calls. I eventually lost my cool after taking yet another phone message for him, and upon knocking on his office door found myself being shouted at for "disturbing him." Four years of pent-up frustration came out in a torrent of vernacular and the following day I found myself being interviewed by "The Management." I explained the background to the event.

"If it has been a problem for so long, why didn't you approach him before?" The irony of all this was too good to be true. An asshole who bricks himself up in his office and shouts at people when disturbed was genuinely surprised that someone found him unapproachable, and hence didn't approach him about his inapproachability. He "retired" a couple of months later.

One curious feature I have noticed with the Right Men I have encountered is that a distorted view of reality develops owing to the way other people relate to him. Other people find that the Right Man is best avoided wherever possible, and will only interact with him when they have little or no other choice, or when they need or want something from him. So to avoid eliciting any of the problems inherent in dealing with the Right Man, it seems common sense to crank up the manners and the charm.

As a result, the Right Man can frequently develop the world view that, "*People are only nice when they want something.*" In working with them, being nice can often be counterproductive, because it elicits distrust and paranoia. On the inside, the Right Man's world must be at least as unpleasant as the results of it on the outside.

Personally, I find the best way to deal with a Right Man is to simply be somewhere else. When they come to me as clients, I happily refer them to a therapist I don't like.

Eluding Resistance

"I close my eyes so that they cannot see me and I keep still so their voices cannot scare me." —Motionless Mary explains her strategy for hiding from psychiatric nurses.

In *Magic In Action*, a book of transcripts of change-work sessions by Richard Bandler, (7) a woman had a problem with "anticipatory loss" that led her into anxiety and panic. Whenever someone was late for an appointment, she'd imagine them being in a car wreck, zoom in on the gore, and freak out.

It's worth noting that this woman was a psychiatric nurse, where this strategy had a certain utility, and she might even have learned it on the job. For instance, if one of your patients doesn't return from the bathroom promptly, it is useful to make images of disturbing possibilities, become anxious about them, and go find out what is going on.

When Bandler asks her what change she wants, she says, *"What I would like to do is distance myself, so that when I'm in the situation that I wouldn't experience the fear to the degree I have it."*

That is a pretty explicit and detailed set of instructions telling Bandler exactly what to do. Often clients will tell you *precisely* what they need, *if* you know what to listen for.

A client of mine, seeking help coming to terms with a messy divorce, said something quite similar. She said to me, "What I'd like is to be able to dissociate myself from my past with my husband, put the memories behind me, forget about them, and move forward with my life."

Again that is a specific set of instructions about what to do. She has unpleasant representations that she is associated into. These are what she'd like to dissociate from and move behind her and forget. This is just too easy.

But how many people would hear this part: "What I'd like is *to be able to*—"? You have to give the instructions in a way that is meaningful and can be easily translated into action. Working in business and health care management, I have met far too many managers who believe that problems are solved by making rules or pronouncements about them rather than specifying exactly how to *do* something different.

All too often the client is not consciously aware of any internal representation other then the resulting intense feelings that they experience. Their language may reveal their internal representation, but not everyone is aware of this. You may make them aware while they are present in your office, but when they are in the context of their problem, their resources to change the representation may evaporate and they will fall back into their problem behaviours.

Now read again the words from *Magic In Action*: "What I would like to do is distance myself so that *when I'm in the situation* that I wouldn't experience the fear to the degree I have it." We also need to pay attention to these contextual distinctions, so that the change becomes available to a client where and when they want it.

Yet another piece is *how* you tell someone to get more distance. Telling a client to *push* a disturbing image away from them presents several possible problems. Firstly, the instruction "*push* it away" implies resistance and difficulty. I had plenty of experiences as a child of pushing other kids away from me when they behaved towards me in a manner that I didn't like. Those kids usually came back at me in a much more unpleasant mood than they were in before. So don't tell the client to "push" the representation away from him. Use some elegance. "*Allow* that image to move away from you" presupposes that it will happen unless they take action to stop it. "What happens when you *slide* that image away from you?" presupposes that it will be easy, because of the word "slide." When you ask him to tell you "What happens?" you are priming him to notice a difference, and you are also giving an indirect suggestion that helps bypass any conscious resistance.

Secondly, the client has probably already tried to do move an image away, albeit unconsciously, and failed. Or the client may already believe that they can't do it. "What I would like to do—" "I would like to be able to—"

Milton Erickson has written about telling an obese client who would like to lose weight to *increase* her weight intentionally. The client knows she can do *that*, she's done that over and over. Then later he would have her reduce to her previous weight. Now the she has a reference experience of losing weight, and can continue reducing.

So before telling someone to slide something away from them, ask them to slide the representation *toward* them first. Here's the deal—when you ask them to slide it away from them, they might find that this is something they are not able to do. Reducing the problem is something they haven't found easy in the past, so why would now be any different?

However, making a problem *worse* is much easier for most; it is something they have invariably done many times before, consciously or otherwise. So you can ask them to slide it *toward* them first, and then notice the difference that makes. "What happens when you slide that representation toward you, so it is about half the distance now?"

Then get them to hold it there for a moment, before you ask them to slide it back to where it was before. I've *never* had a client who could not do this. Yet in doing so they have just slid the representation away from them, without resistance. This creates a new reference experience of ease in moving a representation away from them, which I then capitalise on by having them slide it even *farther* away, so that it is less disturbing.

Another factor is that you need to specify *where* someone moves an image to. For instance, let's say the client has a timeline (2, ch. 1) in the common "in time" configuration, with the past behind them, and their future in front. If they slide the representation a yard away in front of them, what will happen as time passes? As they move through time, they will gradually get closer to the problem again, and it will "return." You need to be specific—both verbally, and nonverbally—about *where* they move their representation.

Try this now; find an unpleasant past experience that is still a bit bothersome and see it in front of you. Give the negative feeling a score of 1-10 for intensity. Now, close your eyes and slide the representation towards you, until it is at the tip of your nose, then slide it through you and out the back, all the way behind you. Open your eyes and think about that past experience again. Chances are high that the intensity will have reduced significantly.

While distance alone usually serves to reduce unpleasant feelings, it is unlikely to create a permanent change, because it doesn't give the client's brain any instruction as to what *else* to do instead. This is where the Swish Pattern (1, ch. 17; 2, ch. 3) can be useful, because the unresourceful representation is replaced with a resourceful self-image.

Without a new alternative, chances are that when the problem arises again, the client's brain will simply resort to the old behavior. This is the classic scenario of the client who feels great in the therapist's office, but reverts to feeling bad when they are back in the context in which they sought to feel and behave differently.

Seeing Red

"Never go to bed mad. Stay up and fight."
—Phyllis Diller

Even after all these years I still get surprised by the referrals I get. I mean, who would think of sending a habitual violent young offender to a hypnotist? Well, it sure is a wide and varied world, and sometimes you *do* find an enlightened social worker.

The referral notes were the size of a phone book, and they didn't make pretty reading. I was advised that I might not want to see him in my own office if I had anything breakable in there. In short, I was to be very wary of him indeed, and to be afraid, *very* afraid.

Now this just isn't my style. I have learned from working in various places that the existing employees all try to induct the new guy into the right way of thinking. If he doesn't conform to the prevailing mindset, he may well find himself excluded from the team. One hospital department I consulted on had the problem of trying to change the overtly negative culture amongst the employees. As people became disgruntled and left, the management would be excited about the prospect of "new blood." However, any attempts at remaining upbeat and positive were rapidly stomped on, as the new employees found themselves being rapidly inducted into the correct way of thinking for that department.

I always refuse to make an appointment until I can speak to the person who actually *wants* the appointment. A colleague has a similar rule. "It makes sure the client *owns* the appointment." While I don't know too much about this kind of ownership, I do know that when I don't speak to the client first, they rarely turn up.

When I spoke to this kid on the telephone he asked if he could bring his mum along. I think he was a bit nervous. And he did turn up—with his mum. This kid, barely 15, and with a criminal record

115

that would make angels weep, arrived clutching his mother as though it was his first day of school. The social worker stepped forward, and said, "This is Darren." That kind of reminded me of real-estate agents who on showing you the kitchen say, "This is the kitchen." We really need to do better than this. Yes, really.

So I'm dressed in my smartest and most formal suit. I sit in the office with mother, Darren and the social worker. I do the formalities and I *am* formal. Also, most important, I completely ignore Darren. We all talk about him as though he isn't there. He seems comfortable with things this way.

Subsequently Mother and social worker are dismissed with instructions to return later. I'll call them. In the meantime, "I'll have a talk with Darren."

I return to my office. Darren is sitting there somewhat disquieted. I remove my jacket and tie casually, and pull out a pack of cigarettes. Having lit one, I toss the packet and lighter *at* Darren. He catches them, watching me for a cue as to whether to light one, say something, or whatever. I give him no such cue.

"You like veal?" I ask, exhaling.

"Errr. . . huh?" He's clearly confused.

"*Veal*. You like it?" He shrugs. He is clearly unsure what is going on here.

"Veal, as you may be aware, comes from baby cows—do you know any baby cows?"

Now he is seriously confused, and very unsure of how to respond. There is no jocularity in my tone and no cue about how to behave. He looks at me, speechless. He's reached that delightful, "Oh shit!" stage.

"And these baby cows, did you know that they blindfold them before they kill them?'

He shrugs.

"Yes. The baby cows die screaming, but because they are blindfolded *they cannot know what they are screaming at.*"

His eyes widen to the size of dinner plates.

"Now, I am a hypnotist, CLOSE YOUR EYES. . . ."

"What happens in your mind just before you lose your temper?"

Frightened people tend to understand words literally, and questions tend to bypass conscious processing altogether.

"I just see red." He replied, eyes still very firmly closed.

"*Just* red?" I enquire. "What else?"

"I don't know," He protested.

"Yes you do," I insist, "What else?"

"I just see their face and the picture is red."

I pull out a fresh chicken from underneath my chair and hold it in front of him. (More than a few students who have come to watch me work have expressed their surprise at such antics. "I didn't think you actually did that kind of thing!" is a common remark.)

"Open your eyes and tell me what I am holding in front of you," I say niccly.

He opens his eyes, blinks for moment in confusion.

"Looks like a chicken," he states, quite correctly.

"Now, close your eyes and see the chicken in your imagination. Can you do that?"

"Yes," he tells me.

"Now begin, *slowly at first*, begin to change that picture of the chicken into the same kind of red picture as when it happens, do it—quickly *now*!"

My video camera was all set up and already recording. I wasn't entirely sure that this was going to work, but I've learned that it's always worth being prepared for these things just in case. It *was* worthwhile, because that kid opened his eyes in a blind rage, snatched that chicken out of my hands and started trying to beat it to death.

His rage lasted less than 2 minutes, but it was *very* clear that to be the target of that level of violence would be a very bad thing indeed. The chicken, previously killed in a humane manner, was thoroughly tenderised.

I ask him, "What happened there?'

"I just saw red," he told me.

"You just saw red," I echoed. "Anything else?" I ask this young man who has just spent two minutes beating a dead chicken.

"I just saw red. . . ." And then that certain special look began to appear on his face as the train of realisation pulled up at the station. He made the connection that it wasn't the chicken that created the reaction, but rather that he did it himself. He also realized that I'd set him up.

"Shit! Fuck! Fuck! Bastard!" He said half angry, half laughing, and half something else.

"You want the chicken back?" I offered, "Or maybe you'd prefer a baby cow this time?'

"Nooooooooooooooooo!! Nooooooooooooooooooooooooo!!" he exclaimed laughing.

"Blindfold?" I offered, equating him to a calf ready for slaughter.

He slumped back in the chair and began to fire a rapid series of questions about how the way he made those pictures created his anger and rage. He was very quick to realise the implications, and very quick to start to see the possibilities.

I quickly rewound the videotape and played him the recording of himself beating up the chicken. Naturally I anchored his embarrassed response by referring to him as "chicken beater." Having him view the tape provided a nice submodality shift to the experience—now he's *watching* himself beating a chicken. In viewing the ridiculous scene of himself assaulting a dead chicken, he is dissociated from the imagery and of course the imagery is smaller, making it less evocative. Additionally, since it is now on a screen, it is also two-dimensional and framed. If I'd wanted to, I could have adjusted the audio qualities, I could fast-forward or rewind it a few times, make it black and white, and so on.

"So, 'chicken beater,' how's it looking?" I asked, getting him to report back from his new perspective. He was almost speechless.

This young man now has a reference experience for moving an image from associated to a dissociated perspective in a way that he can easily understand. I could have taken it further if I'd wanted to, and built in an "observer" perspective by videotaping him as he watched the first video recording. Later I could get him to watch himself reacting to watching himself beating up a chicken. I thought I'd save that for a later session if required.

I showed him further submodality chaining where we transformed irritation to boredom, boredom to excitement, belief to disbelief and so on. He was excited by this, and quickly started asking further questions as to how people can be in better control of their thinking and emotions.

We went through different techniques, questions and answers, and he started to realise that the solutions to the challenges in his life weren't about "being in control" of his temper. He'd probably been told a *lot* in the past that he either lacks control, or needs to learn to control his emotions/temper etc., but they never showed him *how* to do it. It is really not about control, but rather about steering his thinking so that he can feel different emotions that are more useful.

From tossing him the cigarettes, to scaring him with the veal story, through to the submodality changes resulting from the camera, this one brief set of simple therapeutic manoeuvres was all that was required for him to stay out of trouble. Follow-up one year later proved that he was settled into full-time education and was doing well. There had been no serious or untoward incidents since that single session.

The chicken was subsequently cooked with lemon sauce and served with a light fluffy rice and salad.

Hysterical Paralysis

*"And while Tiggers may appear energetic to the extreme,
their love of ceaseless action and sensation is actually a form
of spiritual laziness."*   —Benjamin Hoff

"Hysterical paralysis" used to be quite common, but is now very rare. I can think of two possible reasons: 1. It simply isn't in vogue culturally, so people's brains don't think of doing it, and/or 2. Better diagnostic techniques and medical understanding means that a "differential diagnosis" is often found. What this means is that many people who used to be treated for "hysteria" actually had multiple sclerosis, tumours, or some other neurological disease that was previously unrecognized.

For instance, the "off/on" nature of multiple sclerosis (MS) is still baffling to many people. They often think that someone is somehow faking it, because yesterday a patient couldn't move, and today they are out walking to the shops. I was nursing one MS patient who was admitted to us in a state of nearly total paralysis the previous day. That morning I was washing her and she sneezed and immediately said, "Oh, I'm back!" Full movement had returned, literally in a sneeze. An MS patient could spend years—and a small fortune—in Freudian analysis in a futile search for the unconscious conflict that was causing her "hysteria."

We had one guy admitted to neurosurgery with a left frontal neuroma. It was slow-growing, and had been there for quite some time. When the left frontal lobe is damaged, depression is a common result—and this guy had been in group therapy for over a year exploring the causes of his depression. There were some obvious signs that his depression was secondary to a tumour, but the therapist didn't know the signs, and never thought to check. Treatment for his potentially fatal condition was delayed considerably because of the therapist's lack of knowledge—and he probably never offered him a refund either.

Whilst we have all this neurological strangeness going on, we also estimated that at any one time, up to 50% of our patients on one ward were fakers. At one end of the faking spectrum are the total fraudsters who are often "hospital hoppers," people who just want to be pampered and taken care of, and who vanish as soon as they are exposed. There are many giveaway signs, and one of these is that you can never get them into a scanner. They always have a convulsion on the way down there, or something similar to keep us from finding out that there is nothing wrong. One guy in his 20s, admitted with Guillan-Barre syndrome, was with us for two weeks before a new student arrived on the ward who had been to school with him and knew his background. The guy vanished within minutes, miraculously cured as he ran from the unit.

"Factitious disorder" is surprisingly common, and something all therapists and healers need to know about. My favourite was the one I spent a frustrating afternoon with, who wanted me to cure him of his addiction to therapy. I fell into the trap by giving him an appointment, but that's a story for another time.

At the other end of the faker spectrum are those who are unaware of the "game" they are caught in. It is common for children to somatise emotions with "tummy aches" and such like, and for some this can continue into adulthood. These are termed "conversion reactions," because the psychological discomfort is converted into a physiological response. For instance a stress rash isn't faked; the psychological component or trigger may exist outside of the client's conscious awareness.

What is interesting about many people with psychosomatic disorders and conversion syndromes is how they blissfully deny any disturbance or difficulties in their psychological lives. We had one guy who collapsed one day at work in a state of total bodily weakness. He presented to us in a state of semi-paralysis that defied all neurological patterns and syndromes. After exhaustive tests, it was concluded that this was a conversion syndrome.

Throughout all of this, he was calm and happy and never showed the slightest signs of the frustration or bewilderment that you would expect anyone in that predicament to display. He denied any stress or psychological issues and hurts and was in hospital for about a year before being transferred to a long-stay care unit. Meanwhile, his wife told us that he was a people-pleaser and a doormat and that he was undergoing enormous stresses at work prior to his collapse. A week before his collapse she had told him that she was going to leave him, and was taking the kids and the dog.

Using hypnosis with conversion syndromes is often helpful. Utilize the dissociation, and communicate directly with the part of the body that is expressing the symptoms. You can set up finger signals so that it is the "unconscious mind" or even "the hand"—or whatever part of the body exhibits the problem—that is communicating. What you do next will be guided by what you are presented with. There isn't a prescriptive approach that I am aware of, but if all else fails go back to the dark ages of NLP and consider using:

1. Six-step Reframing. (8, ch. 4) It is antiquated I know, but it didn't stop working when newer methods were developed, or

2. For experienced hands only, abreaction—even more antique, but it is remarkably successful in these—and only these—cases. When someone can express their feelings overtly, then there is no longer any need to "convert" them into physical symptoms.

I recall one patient who was referred to me with a recurring temporary paralysis to her left arm and leg. Neurological investigations confirmed a serious abnormality in the form of an "arterio-venous mass" (AVM) deep within her brain that was causing some problems. There was much debate amongst the neurological team as to the exact cause of the paralysis and the consensus leaned toward thinking that whilst the AVM might be a contributory cause, the psychological nature of the patient and the patterns in the manifestation of the symptoms suggested that the paralysis was psychological in origin.

During the interview to ascertain this lady's history a pattern emerged that I found of interest. From a humble background, she had married a domineering and successful man and easily fell into the role of the supportive housewife whose life and marriage revolved only around the career of her husband. Her husband, a loyal man with a strong sense of duty believed it to be his role to be the all-providing, all-supporting husband and that his wife's role was to look after the home and children. For him, the very idea of his wife working indicated a failure on his part; *he* was the dutiful provider.

In the early years of the marriage this arrangement worked just fine. But as the children grew older and required less attention, and her husband's career demanded more and more of his time away from home, she grew restless. She wanted more independence and to have some of her own money and develop her own interests in the world. But the relationship that she and her husband had built forbade any expression of this.

First came the depression. "Involutional melancholia" was the first diagnosis—meaning that she was miserable and it was due to no obviouis external factor. Such diagnostic terms are a good "get out" clause for everyone involved, including the diagnosing psychiatrist. Next came the anti-depressant medication and sleeping pills. These helped a little, but still the desire to expand her horizons grew.

And then one day, as he was about to leave for another business trip overseas, something strange happened. An odd tingling sensation began to affect her left arm and leg, which rapidly developed into numbness and then into a full paralysis. Understandably, the symptoms alarmed both of them, and the husband took her quickly to the emergency room. Assessment was rapid and after a few hours waiting, she was admitted overnight to the neurological department where the symptoms disappeared during the night. She was discharged later the next day with a series of outpatient appointments for exhaustive investigations. The AVM was quickly identified, but the symptoms of paralysis were not adequately explained by it.

Over the next few months the pattern became evident. "My husband tells me that I only ever get ill when he has to go away," she told me. It was clear that she had not herself noticed a pattern nor connected any of the "dots" between her symptoms and her emotional frustrations.

With her husband present, I put her into a light trance, and she proved to be an excellent trance subject. I began to explain that under hypnosis parts of her mind would be asked to speak *their* truth and to do so would not be *her* responsibility. As the hypnotherapist, I would be responsible for everything that happened during hypnosis, and that nothing said or revealed would be her fault. I used the word "fault" deliberately. Speaking directly to her left arm and leg, I asked them to communicate anything that they had to say about "this woman's" life. My tone of voice on the words, "this woman" was one of derision, and this created a nice dissociation of responsibility, something that because of her symptoms, I know that she can already do.

The effect was both dramatic and surprising. In a scene reminiscent of the movie, "The Exorcist," a voice most unlike her own voice started speaking, saying that she was "spineless," "weak" and "pathetic." The voice suggested many things about the lady's character weaknesses and defective nature. It was wholesale unpleasant. When the voice had finished its tirade, I thanked the arm and leg, and then said to the woman, "I hope you have been listening carefully to that." Clearly she had, because at that moment she opened her eyes and broke down in tears, sobbing wildly. In situations such as this I do not offer tissues or attempt to get the tears to stop. Instead I waited for a couple of minutes and then offered the rather heartless, "Wow, that is quite a reaction! So, how do you feel?"

Of course she felt dreadful, and it was this dreadful feeling that had gone unrecognised by her consciously for too long. She had chosen to ignore it and "stuff it down" in order to continue living her life according to the now outdated rules of her marriage. Looking over to her husband, I saw that he, too, was crying. I learned later that this was the first time that he'd ever shown any "real emotion" in front of his wife. Seizing the opportunity, I looked back at the lady and indicating her husband's newly-found emotional state, I jokingly said, "Look there! Now see what you have done!"

And that was pretty much all I needed to do. Suggesting that it was a good time for them to talk, I left the room to go and make a cup of tea and read the newspaper. They were able to sort through the rest themselves; they just needed permission to do it.

The AVM continued to exert its problems and was later removed successfully by the skilled neurosurgical team. However from the single brief abreactive hypnosis session the couple grew closer emotionally, and the paralysis disappeared.

Binds

"Time is the great physician"
—Benjamin Disraeli

From The Hypnosis Training Manual

A Bind is a presupposition that gives an illusion of choice, for example: "Would you prefer tea or coffee?" The question is not, "Would you like a drink?" The question presupposes that the client will take *either* tea or coffee.

There are four possible responses the client can give, and each will give an indication of further responsiveness:
1. "Tea, please." (staying within scope of the bind)
2. "Coffee, please." (staying within scope of the bind)
3. "Neither, thanks." or simply, "No" (rejecting the bind)
4. "Are you having one?" (seeking permission)

"Would you like to go into trance slowly, or would you like to really take your time and enjoy the process of going into trance?" presupposes going into trance by directing attention to the alternative ways of going into trance. In reality, both choices are actually the same. The context (a fee-paying client for a hypnosis session) means that the client is unlikely to reject the bind by saying, "I don't want to go into trance at all." Of course, occasionally a client will seek permission and ask the hypnotist for guidance, "How do you think I should go into trance?" Which of course makes the rest very easy.

In English there are three types of sentence based on intonation:
1. Questions end with an *upward* inflection.
2. Statements end *without* inflection.
3. Commands end in a *downward* inflection.

125

In the West, raised eyebrows are an indication for the other person to respond and say something. Policemen know this, and they know how to use it in interviews. An ex-policeman friend once told me of the power of the raised eyebrow. "The subject will answer with minimal information then look at you with raised eyebrows as though to say, 'Is that OK?' All we do is look back at him, straight-faced, and raise our eyebrows and keep them raised. He'll always start to feel uncomfortable and will quickly supply the extra details without any other prompting."

You can also influence the option that the client chooses by the appropriate use of language. For example, to encourage the client to choose coffee, you could say, "Would you like tea, or would *you prefer coffee*." Or even, "Perhaps you might like tea, or *you will choose a cup of coffee*." The italics indicate an embedded command, marked out by emphasis. Notice that there are no question marks in those sentences. They are said with a *downward* inflection, indicating a command. The client's choice can be further influenced using tonality by saying, "tea" in a tone of depression or disgust, and "coffee" in a tone of pleasure or excitement. And if you raise your eyebrows, that is a further cue to respond, which is also a subtle command.

Brain Cancer

"Will it hurt?"
—Neuro-surgical patient about to receive a pain-killing injection.

I don't usually take referrals when a client's relative makes the appointment on their behalf. Experience tells me that too many times out of 100, that client will not show up. If they are too shy to speak to me on the phone, then they are likely to be positively terrified to actually turn up in person—especially knowing some of the stunts I've pulled on clients.

However when Jane's mother called me, I sensed a difference. Her mum told me that Jane, an intelligent 29-year-old social worker had woken up in a state of morbid fear on Monday. The fear had been severe enough for her to call her mother, who had immediately travelled the 80-mile round trip to bring her daughter home with her. Four days later—despite the hefty doses of diazepam administered by the GP—her state of intense anxiety continued to grow. The GP was becoming sufficiently concerned to consider taking Jane into hospital for assessment.

Taking a little medical history, I learned that nine years previously, Jane had undergone neurosurgery to remove a tumour from the nerve of her left ear. Other than this, there was no other psychiatric, medical, or surgical history of note.

A neurolemmoma, or schwannoma, is a non-cancerous growth that occurs on the nerve leading from the inner ear to the brain. This particular nerve has two parts, one associated with transmitting sound, while the other sends information to the brain from the balance organs of the inner ear. These tumours can be quite small (a half-inch to an inch), are slow-growing, and most are diagnosed in people aged 30-60. Surgery to remove them is invariably successful, although hearing loss to the affected ear and facial weakness can

127

occur. Occasionally the paralysis will be severe enough that the eyelid on the affected side of the face will need to be stitched closed to keep the eye from drying out. However, strangely there appears to be a nonlinear relationship between cutting the facial nerve and facial paralysis. Sometimes patients will develop a paralysis without the nerve being cut and vice versa. Before 1960, the majority of patients developed a facial paralysis. However, the percentage is steadily declining as advances in surgical technique develop.

Just under nine years after her tumour was removed, Jane did not understand the cause of her fear but she certainly understood *what* she was scared of.

"I feel like I'm about to die," she told me. "Actually, I *know* I'm about to die really soon, but I don't know *how* that I know."

On taking Jane's particulars on the telephone her mum had told me the date of the neurosurgery—December 13—nine years previously. Today was December 11. I somehow suspected that this was not a coincidence.

"What happened . . .?" I asked slowly, as I changed the focus of my eyes, deepening my breathing as I led Jane into a calmer state, and she followed.

"Hmmmm?" she responded.

"What happened, . . . when the doctor told you that you had a brain tumour?" I used the words "brain tumour" rather than acoustic neuroma. Hospital staff are notorious at speaking a different language—on hearing "acoustic neuroma" or "glioblastoma multiform" or "left frontal benign space-occupying lesion" the patient will ask for a translation—but no matter how well the professional tries to shield it, the translation that the client makes is simply, "brain cancer" and as we all know, "brain cancer" is bad.

"I thought, 'This is it, I'm going to die' and I told the surgeon I was scared I was going to die. He told me that I wasn't going to die if I had the operation, but the operation could leave me permanently disfigured and deaf in one ear."

Legal and medical ethics state that doctors have to get "informed consent" before they can operate. Essentially what this means is that they have to terrify the patient with all the possibilities of what can go wrong, as well as what can go right.

Deepening my own state, with both Jane and her mother following me, I encouraged Jane to go on, "And then, what did he say?"

"I just freaked out" she said calmly, "I just lost it completely. It was all too much." That is, she was pushed through threshold, into a state in which she was *supremely* open to suggestion.

"Then what happened?" I asked, "What happened next?"

"He told me quite sternly that my choice was simple, I'd either have a facial drop or I'd be dead within nine years. It was up to me."

It was the "It was entirely up to me (to choose between disfigurement or death)" that alarmed me most. Such choices are not made easily. Once I had an elderly patient with penile cancer; he had the choice to retain his genitals and die, or lose them and extend his survival. His reasoning was simple; at 85, he would probably not live that much longer anyway, and he would rather do so accompanied by a penis that had served him well throughout his life. So you can imagine that to present a young woman, still reeling from the shock of hearing that she had *brain cancer*, with the devil's choice between death and disfigurement was clearly just too much.

And so there we had it. Because very clearly, sitting there right in front of me was a healthy 29-year-old woman, who had undergone successful neurosurgery, and who owing to the skill of the neurosurgeon had neither eye droop, hearing loss, nor more importantly, any sign of facial paralysis.

Focused, aroused, and in a highly suggestible state, she heard the doctor tell her that she could potentially suffer facial disfigurement or die. So now without any facial disfigurement, that left only one choice.

"So, when are you *supposed* to die?" I asked.

"Thursday!" Jane said spontaneously, with a more than just a hint of surprise.

"*This* Thursday?" I asked, encouraging her down this line of logic.

"Oh my God!" she exclaimed as she touched her face, "That's ridiculous!" And right then and there she developed a facial drop and some numbness. I hadn't planned for this, but it appeared that her unconscious had remade its choice. It only took a little further work to resolve this using a little timeline work and "change history" patterning. Follow-up one year later revealed no anxiety relapse—nor any facial paralysis or numbness.

r

The Dead Guy

"Was that really necessary?"
—First words spoken by a resuscitated patient, immediately after
receiving successful defibrillation.

Something that interests me is the number of men I have met
who had a personal timeline that terminated on a specific date. This
date is usually the age that their father died prematurely from a heart
attack. For example, one guy was certain that he would die when he
was 54, since this was the age that both his father and his grandfather
dropped dead. When he didn't die, he actually seemed a bit disappointed. However, I doubt these guys consciously think, "OK, I am
going to die on February 12, when I am 54," so I always ask, "What
time exactly is this heart attack going to happen?"

One patient of mine had received a very successful Coronary
Artery Bypass Grafting (CABG, or in hospital speak "cabbage"),
which is essentially surgery that plumbs veins around the blockages or
narrowing in the arteries in the heart. The problem was that this guy
was told that the grafting would be good for 5 years. Surgery was successful, and his quality of life soared. As time passed and the five years
was up, no matter how physically fit he was, or how many diagnostic
tests were returned with an "all clear" (the grafts were clear, unblocked
and his heart was in great shape) the fact still remained that he had
been told that they would be good for 5 years, and he assumed that
meant that they would *only* be good for five years. Now that those five
years were over, he was living on "borrowed time." He became a regular face at our clinic—sometimes twice a day—demanding that we
take his blood pressure. He demanded to see the calibration certificates
over and over, and he recorded every conversation that occurred. His
pedantry was phenomenal. From a holiday destination on which he

took with him a qualified nurse—"just in case"—he sent me a post-card that simply said, "On holiday with my nurse. I dream of death."

No amount of reassurance and reasonable suggestion that he was wrong was of help—in his world-view, anyone who reassured him clearly did not know what they were talking about, and he'd write it down in his ever-present little notebook to be reported back to his long-suffering general practitioner.

I decided that professionalism be damned, I had to do something about this. I was beginning to dread going into work knowing that this pedantic asshole would be showing up and giving me a hard time every day. For some reason, in hospitals "professionalism" means that you should never lose your cool or shout or demonstrate any neg-ative or hostile emotion towards any patient or client. To this, I just have to ask, "Why the hell not?"

As a nursing student, I had a patient once who would punish the staff for being late with his dinner tray by dropping his trousers in the middle of the ward and taking a shit right there in the corridor. He would often pick up some of it and throw it at members of staff. This man had been bullying the staff since his arrival. Apparently he found this funny, and he could do this because he "paid his taxes" and it would "teach the nurses a lesson." If I'd been in charge, I'd have slung his fat ass out of the hospital there and then, and let him sort out his health problems himself. But the difficulty with this approach is that these people have legal "rights" which they are very happy to invoke at great speed when it suits them.

"Well, I'll be damned!" I said to the blood pressure guy. "You *are* going to die and it looks like you are going to die *today*!" I imme-diately asked him to quickly leave the clinic, since if he died outside, then it would be someone else's responsibility to deal with the body and not mine.

"You aren't taking me seriously" he whined.

"Get out! Get out!" I insisted, and ushered him out the door. He left the clinic muttering something about putting forward an official complaint. I told him dead people can't complain, and sent him on his way. He never actually put through the complaint but he did con-tinue to come to the clinic, so I started calling him "The Dead Guy," and would say things such as, "Hey man, you are looking good today for a dead guy! Hey, it's The Dead Guy, hope you are not smelling too bad today."

"Hi Andy," he said, "How you doing?"

"I'm doing good," I reply, "But hey, tell me, are you still going to be The Dead Guy in 5 years time?"

"I guess so," says he.

"And are you still going to be The Dead Guy in 10 years time?"

"Umm, . . . I guess so."

"That's great!" I continue, "So, you are going to be The Dead Guy forever! Cool!" and I ushered him back out of the clinic without reference to his blood pressure or any of the usual palaver.

I kept this going until the joke got boring, and he asked me to stop. By this point, he was over his obsession, because my endless joking about it made it into an irritation.

The Tinfoil Helmet

"Though this be madness, yet there is method in it."
—William Shakespeare

I have found that when I work directly with the submodalities of a schizophrenic's voices, a decent level of trance helps tremendously, but isn't essential. Of course the process of changing submodalities is itself an excellent trance induction, and schizophrenics are no more or less susceptible than anybody else. It does frighten the psychiatrists though, who feel far more comfortable with a prescription pad and cozy office chair. For some reason they are afraid to hypnotise schizophrenics, psychotic depressives, and epileptics, which I find very strange indeed. Now any halfway decent NLP practitioner will already know how to do auditory submodality changes (You do, don't you?) so there is little for me to add here, but here are a couple of tips that you may not have thought of:

1. Reducing the volume of a voice won't necessarily improve it for the schizophrenic. This is especially true for a suspicious paranoid who may be hearing "whispering" voices, so increasing the volume may be of benefit there. Slowing the voice right down is one of the best trance inducers I have seen. However while getting the client to relax is a valuable thing—you must consider the issue of suggestibility. If he goes away, hears voices, slows them down and trances out—what suggestions might he be vulnerable to? Psychiatric professionals aren't exactly the best "positive frame" hypnotists on the planet. One bozo I worked with would ask the depressives every day, "Any suicidal thoughts today?" and if they said "No," he would invariably tag them with, "Are you sure?"

Asking the question, "Any suicidal thoughts today?" immediately refocuses the patient onto the negative. "Are you sure?" questions the

133

patient's experience, and effectively communicates disapproval for *not* having thought anything suicidal that day. It also makes the staff an anchor for thinking of suicide, and sets up an expectation set whereby the client may well find it easier to report suicidal thoughts rather than face disbelief.

As a very young child I remember well the experience of being accused in school of having stolen a child's pen on the first day of a new school. The teacher's behaviour made it clear that he was in no doubt that I had indeed stolen it. The other children were thus cued into immediate hostility towards me. Somehow I knew that the safest option would be to agree with the accusation and apologise, rather than be thought of as a thief *and* a liar.

We already know that the patient was admitted for suicidal ideation (two *years* previously!) so it seemed odd to keep reinforcing and building upon this. The problem is that when you are a psychiatric patient, your diagnosis and medical file tends to follow you—or even precede you—everywhere you go. I proposed that we let go of the reasons for admission, since that was history, and instead concentrate on building a different kind of *future*—one that preferably didn't involve a recurrent investigation of the negative.

2. Pay attention to the client's *external* speaking voice. Many schizophrenics (and many other clients, too) only have one speaking voice with a fixed tempo, tonality, volume, etc., regardless of the content or context—what is often called "flat affect." If they are unable to introduce variation into their speaking voice, the same is likely to be true on the inside too. One Christmas, I took a schizophrenic lady with a very loud and toneless voice singing carols. We all endured a few torturous days of her singing badly at the top of her voice before she was able to start to tune up a little. By getting her to pay attention to the other singers, she was able to build a model of a much softer and nicer voice, and I used this as a reference experience when making internal submodality changes. The biggest impact of this was on her overall demeanour—with a calmer and more melodic speaking voice, she calmed down a great deal. Other staff noticed the change but didn't really understand it. The nurse in charge enthusiastically entered in the notes, "Appears to be responding well to music therapy." (As far as I could tell "music therapy" consisted of

little more than a group of people sitting in a circle mournfully bashing tambourines.)

3. Voice hearing is often not quite so straightforward. For example, one gentleman I worked with wore a tinfoil helmet (yes, he really did) because he wanted to protect himself from the fact that Uranus was putting thoughts into his head. I asked him if the helmet helped at all. "Not much" he told me. I mused aloud if maybe the foil wasn't thick enough. "Good point," he agreed, and he set about looking for more foil to reinforce his helmet.

Now in situations like these you need to decide just where you tap with your therapeutic hammer. Is it the voices in his head that are the problem, or the fact that he believes that Uranus is putting them there, or is it his certainty about it that is the problem?

While this patient worked on reinforcing his helmet, a particularly cool colleague stuck his head out of the window and shouted at the sky, "You arsehole! Leave this poor bastard alone, you hear me? You leave him alone!" I couldn't help but notice the "Uranus" > "Your anus" > "Arsehole" transition, which was probably unconscious, but incredibly appropriate. God only knows what the neighbours thought.

For reasons that I've never really understood, after that the patient never once complained about Uranus bothering him again, and he discarded the helmet the following day. "Here, you take it" he said to me, "It'll help you stop waving your arms about when you talk."

A Mouth Full

"If I had only known, I would have been a locksmith."
—Albert Einstein

As a nursing student, I had to complete a module of community nursing in my local catchment area. Ostensibly this involves visiting housebound patients at home to administer essential nursing services for the community. In reality it involved little more than dressing nasty looking leg ulcers and visiting mad old people who owned a thousand cats. The cat people seemed to have a tendency to sit in a chair all day and all night and their district nurse was often their only lifeline to hygiene and basic relief from pressure sores. The sagely advise I was given prior to visiting these patients was simply, "Son, be careful where you sit, and for God's sake don't drink the tea!"

On one occasion we visited a family whose eight-year-old son had a problem with "chronic psychogenic constipation." What this mouthful of a diagnosis translates into is that he couldn't shit, and they couldn't find a reason why. The poor kid was subjected to twice-weekly high enemas and would be restrained in the living room while the nurse gave the enema. My discomfort at this was increased when it was announced that I would be the one to deliver the ghastly deed, while the nurse and the mother would pin him down on the sofa. Apparently this was the normal way that this sort of thing was done. I just knew that this wasn't going to be good.

Now, the because of the character of the passage that follows, those readers who are eating their lunch right now might want to put this book down and read it a bit later.

What ensued was an appalling struggle, culminating in me delivering the enema. The basic premise of this absurd process is that the enema is given; it works its magic in the child's colon before the child has to make a mad dash up to the bathroom to use the toilet.

But what happened next is one of those experiences that only a nurse would get the privilege of experiencing. The pressurised liquid came squirting appallingly back out and straight into my mouth, but neither mother nor nurse witnessed this, as they were busy pinning down a struggling and very unhappy child.

This was one of those awful moments when time stands still, and you really wish it didn't! Much like when I crashed my motor-cycle, something happened just so that I was fully able to take in the entire horror of the situation and really get my value.

Moments before I actually hit the wall, I just knew that it was going to hurt badly. Then much to my surprise, I can remember thinking to myself, "Oh, that wasn't so bad after all." As I paid closer attention, I realised that the crash hadn't actually finished yet, and that I was still heading toward the wall. The entire impact between front-wheel hitting the wall then me hitting the wall could not have lasted for more than one full second and yet the clarity of my thought suggested an entirely different time frame. And yes, it did hurt. A *lot*.

As I stood there helplessly trapped by my terribly proper middle class upbringing, I gazed in a stupor around the room while my brain struggled to resolve the "spit or swallow" debate. As I looked around the room, every previously ignored detail came stunningly into focus. The carpet was a light cream colour and was immaculate, without so much as a smudge, and quaint plastic sheeting covered all the furniture. There was no dust in any corner or crevice and not a single item was out of place. I imagined that they had white towels and those little scented blocks of hand soap in the bathroom too, *and* I bet that those flannels were ironed and changed every day. It is amazing how much detail it is possible to take in when your brain is writhing and screaming for someone—*anyone*—to please *do* something.

Now here was my realisation—I actually contemplated *swallowing* this horror. Think about it—I have a mouthful of something unmentionable, and I *actually considered swallowing it*. The house was so unbelievably immaculate and upper-class that I was scared to just spit it out onto the floor. It just seemed so incongruous and such a wrong thing to do, and yet I wasn't merely 8 years old—I was a strapping and fine-looking 19-year-old who really should have known better. All the unpleasantness of this situation did make me wonder if maybe, just *maybe*, the problem was simply that the child was afraid to take a shit lest he make a mess. God only knows all the fussing about cleanliness that must have gone on inside that house every day. Subsequent conversation with the district nurses confirmed that now that I had mentioned it and pointed it out, that maybe this *was* the problem. This new perspective didn't change anything though—to add to his developmental traumas, the child was eventually given an anal stretch in that oh-so-helpful way. I have no doubt that the house continued along with its immaculate deception unabated.

Now, if you think that is bad, several years later I got into a heated argument with a child psychiatrist with regard to her treatment of a precociously intelligent and physically developed 11-year-old girl with "asthma." This young patient had spent more than 90% of the previous 7 months as an in-patient on the medical unit. Despite all negative clinical findings, each time she was discharged home the girl would inevitably end up back in the emergency room to be readmitted.

Steroids were administered, allergy tests were completed, psychiatric evaluations performed, but the situation never changed and all the tests proved negative. Since she never had a single symptom while on the ward, the pattern soon became obvious to everyone involved in her care. Several months into this saga and in response to a direct question (possibly the first of its kind) the girl announced that she thought that the symptoms were the result of her father "raping" her "with his mind."

The social workers went into overdrive and "investigations" into the family were carried out. The girl was examined for signs of abuse. Nothing—the girl was a virgin and the family declared normal. The psychiatrist was clearly at a loss, and diagnosed the girl as having "Post Pubescent Conversion Reaction" The staff all carried on as though this now explained everything. Diagnosis in hand, they gave this 11-year-old child her daily dose of Prozac as though a change in her serotonergic synaptic function would alter everything. It was shortly after this that the staff grew weary of her omnipresence on the ward and declared that she was simply "addicted to hospitals" and subsequently their benevolence towards her began to dry up. They did continue to give her the daily Prozac though.

Now I know it seems strange, but with experiences like this in my background, to be invited to a house to hypnotise a freshly showered obese woman in a dressing gown didn't strike me as being particularly strange. Oh come on, we were all naïve once, right? OK, maybe I should have paid attention to the fact that she was always so keen to mention that her husband was away "at sea" but I didn't. You see how easy it is to miss what is exactly right there in front of you? At least if I ever get a client with "psychogenic constipation," I'll remember to ask what colour their carpets are. It's all about learning.

So I asked her to take a deep breath and relax deeper as I counted back from 10 to 1. By the time I had counted back to 4 I lifted her hand and elicited a most perfect catalepsy. The trance came easy, but now I had a problem—I had absolutely no idea what to do next. I remembered a story a famous hypnotist told once of an early client he saw with dermatitis. He simply gave the ludicrous suggestion that the dermatitis would just go away on it's own, and sure enough it did. How the client managed to translate that suggestion into a physiological response I may never really understand, but I thought that maybe such a technique was worth a shot.

"And as you drift ever deeper into trance, you can find yourself losing weight only at the time and rate that is totally appropriate for you." And that was it. Not really knowing what else to say, I simply left her in trance for the rest of the obligatory 50-minute hour, read the newspaper, and then woke her up and went home. I did exactly the same every week for 6 weeks.

Today, despite the ambiguity of the word "time," I still don't understand what really happened in her mind, but in the absence of any other suggestion or behavioural change, within 3 months her weight had reduced to her ideal level (which I had never actually remembered to ask her about previously). Telephone contact a year later elicited an invitation for dinner and confirmation that her weight had indeed remained stable at her ideal level.

Another obese client had a most remarkable problem. Despite horrendous obesity, this lady didn't appear to be doing anything out of the ordinary to contribute to her excess weight. She was large enough that I feared for my reclining trance chair, so to avoid potential collapse and injury, I had her sit on a large beanbag, which immediately burst. I took a fairly detailed history about diet and exercise, family history, and trends in weight, health etc. All normal. However, looking at the photographs I had asked her to bring, it was clear that her vast increase in body mass had only occurred since she had married. I suspected something was going on there, but I never was very good at playing detective.

"Now close your eyes, deeply, and tell me what is REALLY going on. . . NOW!" I commanded. She blinked, blushed and then put her head in her hands and said, *"I cannot tell, I'm so embarrassed!"*

"Embarrassment be damned," I told her, *"Just tell me now, or I'm getting the whip!"*

And so she told me that she ate a tub of margarine a day; sometimes spread thickly on bread, sometimes just with a spoon.

"Arrgghh . . . what did you tell me that for!" I joked with her, while trying to abate my nausea.

"Dare I ask why you do this?" I ventured, hoping for a reason.

"Oh God!" she said, "I don't believe I've been so stupid." She looked back down again into another altered state, and sat there thinking to herself for about 20 minutes. I just sat there quietly and stared at her. She was clearly reflecting on something important, and it would have been rude to interrupt. When she looked up at me, I raised my eyebrows. She told me that if she lost weight she believed that her husband would leave her. The logic embedded in that statement may not be apparent, because it left quite a few blanks to fill in.

Early in their courtship period, being young and attractive and rather highly sexed, her *husband-to-be* told her categorically that if she were ever to be unfaithful, he would leave her immediately. Knowing her vulnerabilities well, this understandably concerned her a little bit. By being so fat she had effectively rendered herself unattractive to other men, and thus any temptation to stray from her marriage was nullified. We could summarise her situation as, "I eat margarine so I won't be unfaithful." This strategy was an entirely unconscious activity that seemed to surprise her as much as it did me, and it occurred, as with many problem behaviours, in a trance-like state. Having realized what was going on, she could develop other choices about preserving her marriage.

Reframing

"Suppose you try and tell me what you think is wrong.
"I turned the words over suspiciously, like round,
sea-polished pebbles that might suddenly put out
a claw and change into something else.
"What did I think was wrong?
"That made it sound as if nothing was really wrong,
I only thought it was wrong."
—Sylvia Plath, The Bell Jar.

For years I suffered severe anxiety and sought help from a variety of sources, including NLP practitioners and hypnotherapists. Without fail, every single one gave me the same unhelpful line of bullshit. They all told me that anxiety is really just excitement by a different name, and that the physiology and neurology of anxiety and excitement were actually identical—studies proved this, you see? Perhaps that works for some people, but I was still scared shitless—and showed it—but they didn't seem to notice. Really, just what is wrong with these people?

Reframing the meaning of someone else's communication in this way is rarely helpful and is a key pattern in Bateson's model of schizogenesis. (10) It is also, quite frankly, *rude*. Reframing is *not* about invalidating a person's model of the world; reframing a person's meaning in this way demonstrates neither understanding nor competency.

Robert Dilts produced a fine set of patterns he called, "Sleight of Mouth" (19) an understanding that provides an excellent way to track logical reframes in arguments and negotiation. I have also used them for tracking patterns in psychotic communication when working with schizophrenia. The key difference with Dilts' patterns is that Sleight of Mouth patterns don't strip out the meaning of the other

141

person's communication. Instead, they accept that and leave it intact, and then offer a logical extension into a different and possibly more beneficial direction. "Because *that* is true, *this* must *also* be true."

Invalidating a patient's worldview occurred on a regular basis in one of the psychiatric units in which I worked. One schizophrenic guy who was recently admitted to the department was surprised to find that when he told a member of staff that the CIA were monitoring him, he replied quite forcefully, "Don't give me that crap, you idiot, you are just behaving psychotically again." Initially, I was curious to witness this stark refusal to play the psychotic patient's game, but on further observation it became apparent that while the psychotic behaviours and communication decreased around this particular staff member, they continued unabated elsewhere. The patient simply learned to avoid this particular individual, and when in his company preferred to lie about his ongoing experience. This lack of feedback from patients led to the staff member formulating a world-view in which he believed that his approach was highly effective in creating shifts in schizophrenic behaviours. He was widely considered by most staff to be both incompetent and a bully, so naturally it was not long before he was promoted to management.

Another nurse at the same unit had an interesting pattern of reframe that reflected her dedication to the biological model of psychiatry. Any apparent psychotic communication was usually responded to with the tangential and stock answer of, "Have you taken your medication today?" If the client said "Yes" this was generally followed up with, "Are you sure?" The patient's communication was first misconstrued as simply a lack of medication, and then doubt cast on the patient's memory!

Gregory Bateson and Jurgen Ruesch (11) defined tangential communication as:

> The reply inadequately fits the original statement.
> The reply responds to an aspect of the statement that is incidental.
> The reply has a frustrating effect.
> The reply is not directed to the intention behind the original statement, as it is perceivable through word, action and context of the situation.

The effect of this woman's tangential communication was immediately demonstrable when I plotted the rates of the "PRN" madication against the staff timetable. PRN stands for Pro Re Nata— *as the situation demands*; as needed. This is additional medication that the nurses can give without asking the doctor every time. A typical prescription may read, "PRN: Up to 80 mgs. in divided doses in 24 hours as required." So if a patient has had his full quota of standard medication and is still being a nuisance, the nurse is permitted to give additional doses according to the PRN recommendation.

I proffered two explanations for the dramatic rise in PRN druggings whenever this woman was on shift: 1. She just liked drugging people, or 2. There was a demonstrable increase in psychotic behaviours whenever she was on shift. As the unit prided itself on its standardisation of care and professional standards, I was assured that no patient would ever be drugged unless s/he displayed an objective and measurable list of requisite symptoms. Therefore the mere presence of this member of staff must be driving some patients crazy. A personal view, I know, but I would have been happy to see her strangled, or alternatively doped with industrial strength thorazine. Either action would have resulted in a calming effect on everyone around her.

Despite these heretical views on the apparent standardisation of psychiatric care, there is actually a weighty body of evidence and research, albeit "controversial," to suggest that some psychotic behaviours are directly attributable to specific patterns in communication from other people, often caregivers.

A patient might say, "I am made of glass," to which the reply would be, "Have you taken your medication today?" What occurs here is a pattern consistent with Bateson's model of the "double bind'—a common pattern in schizogenesis. Bateson had a complex description of the double bind that has not held up well under scrutiny (10, ch. 9) However Bateson also had a much simpler definition based on incongruence:

> The general characteristics of this [double bind] situation are the following:
> (1) When the individual is involved in an intense relationship; that is, a relationship in which he feels it is vitally

important that he discriminate accurately what sort of message is being communicated so that he may respond appropriately.

(2) And, the individual is caught in a situation in which the other person in the relationship is expressing two orders of message and one of these denies the other.

(3) And, the individual is unable to comment on the messages being expressed to correct his discrimination of what order of message to respond to, i.e., he cannot make a metacommunicative statement. (10, p. 208)

All too often psychiatric professionals fail to understand the effect of the power differential in the relationship between them and the client/patient. Their social position alone imposes a powerful logical retyping of the communication offered. In addition, they are obligated to play two contradictory roles, helper and jailer. This incongruence provides a background meaning for everything they say.

One example of a reframe to the statement, "I am made of glass" that initially interested me as being somewhat different from the norm was, "No, that's just how you *feel*." This was often followed up with such sagely advise as, "So, why don't you have a cup of tea and sit down." However, I soon discovered that in reality the staff only said this because they didn't know what else to say.

It seems that many stock responses from members of psychiatric teams to the behavioural patterns observed in their charges are not based so much on standardisation, but only reflects the local culture within the organisation. In order to be considered a good professional in the eyes of one's peers, you need to demonstrate that you fit in well with the local culture of the organization, whether or not you get results. A member of staff who dares to be outrageous and think innovatively and creatively can put his career progression in serious jeopardy.

That aside for the moment, let us consider some non-tangential responses to the statement "I am made of glass." First, I would consider the context in which the communication occurred. If, as a psychiatric professional, I greeted a hebephrenic schizophrenic with an opening gambit of, "Good morning, how are you today?" should I really be at all surprised if they reply, "I am made of glass"? After all, such a response is quite contextually appropriate. As Profound Peter, the Residential Philosopher of Misery, once commented to me, "Why do these God damn staff get so excited every time someone gets a bit crazy around here? It's a psychiatric hospital, not a freaking nursery!"

Now, just what are the *qualities* of a person made of glass? What kind of glass might they be? If it's cut-crystal then we have a very different situation that if someone is a cheap, chipped beer glass. What are the other qualities of glass? Is the glass clear or opaque? There is very little privacy in any psychiatric institution, as Hawking Harry demonstrated well when he shouted at a staff member performing the hourly "checks," "For *Christ's sake*, what does a guy need to do to have a *private* wank around here? Now fuck off and let me finish!"

So maybe someone made of glass is lacking privacy; everything they do is transparent. Or maybe they feel fragile? Or broken? Or maybe *all* of these possibilities and more besides, being communicated at multiple levels simultaneously. After months of 24/7 psychiatric scrutiny, might you not feel a little shattered?

But then, are such delusions really so transparent?

The "Yes" Set

From The Hypnosis Training Manual
To build rapport and encourage agreement and compliance, begin communication or negotiation using questions that elicit a series of "Yes" responses. Ask questions or make statements that can only have a "Yes" response. The "Yes" response does not need to be verbal, but can simply be a nonverbal agreement. Aim to get five "Yes" responses. The listener will get used to saying "Yes," and will have a tendency to agree with whatever you say next.

"Where are you from?" *"Southampton."* "So, you are from Southampton, is that right?"

You need to demonstrate understanding of the client's model of the world and social position.

"OK, so you made it here today, didn't you, in order to begin to make some changes in your life. Is that right?" This will help build trust and rapport, and establish your position as change agent.

"Yes Set" questions typically include a "tag" negation on the question or statement.

"You have thought about this problem for some time, . . . haven't you?

  . . . didn't you?
  . . . won't you?
  . . . wouldn't you?
  . . . can't you?
  . . . shouldn't you?
  . . . couldn't you?
  . . . mustn't you?

The tag creates an ambiguity in the question, and consequentially in the client's response—is s/he saying "Yes" to the first question, or to the negation in the tag?

The negation can also occur in the first question, rather than in the tag.

"I know that you wouldn't want to go home today without really experiencing a really comfortable trance, would you?"

While using the "yes set" and "tag questions" can undoubtedly enhance compliance in communication, it can also be quite a hindrance when used in a clearly manipulative way by a salesman or someone else who may not be thinking about your best interests. How many of us, I wonder, have felt coerced into agreeing with somebody, or unreasonably manipulated into going along with a particular point of view?

Since all hypnotic language patterns also occur in everyday speech, the hypnosis and NLP language models can help us recognize when that is happening. For example, while watching a movie, the guy turns to his date and says—in a gross violation of e-prime (12)— "This film is terrible, isn't it?"

Notice that the guy didn't say, "I am not enjoying this film." His statement puts his *subjective* experience "out there" as an *objective* fact, and attempts to draw his girlfriend into his version of reality, his trance. Most people have great difficulty in measuring anything objectively. They often measure events not by the event itself, but rather by their *reaction* to them. The assumption is made that everyone measures the event the same way, and anyone who doesn't is wrong, mistaken, or clearly insane.

But actually, the girl was quite enjoying the film, and now she has a problem. Now she has a choice—to invalidate her own experience and agree with him, or disagree with him and take the consequences, what is often called a double bind.

A secretary in an office complex in which I used to work was the hypnotic queen when it came to time distortion. This secretary was an impressive weapon of misery. Dissatisfied in her work, but unwilling to do anything about it, she would wander over to her victim and tag them with, "It's really dragging today isn't it? Don't you just hate it when a boring day goes by so *slowly*?"

For fun we would send her over to another office full of unsuspecting victims. She'd tag them with subjective statements much like our cinema guy, and then immediately follow up with another that the victim is most likely to agree with. For instance:

"We *do* all hate it when a boring day goes by so slowly, don't we? Don't you wish you could go somewhere really nice on holiday instead?"

"It's really hot and stuffy in here, isn't it? Don't you wish they got us proper air conditioning?"

"Why doesn't this photocopier ever work properly? The noise it makes is really annoying, isn't it? They really should get us a new one, shouldn't they?"

"This book is really interesting, isn't it? You really want to tell your friends about it, don't you?" Now.

Voodoo Science

"The supreme satisfaction is to be able to despise one's neighbor and this fact goes far to account for religious intolerance. It is evidently consoling to reflect that the people next door are headed for hell." —Aleister Crowley

Several years ago a successful businessman, who for all appearances was perfectly normal, consulted me. His wife had recently left him, and he was suffering from severe insomnia brought about by issues relating to the separation, and from the demands of his busy work schedule. I took a full history from him and nothing seemed out of the ordinary. He was just a normal guy reacting to his circumstances in a normal way—until I asked him a question I often ask, "So out of all the people in the phone book, why did you come to see me. What is it you think I can do for you?" Dr. Siebert would be proud of me.

"Well," he said, "I know of your interest in the occult, and that is why I thought you could help me. My wife has a friend who is a Black Witch. She is able to enter my mind and make me ill. She is a very powerful woman."

Now, I ask the reader to stop for a moment and think carefully about how you would respond to this. Read the sentence again. Is he mad? Deluded? Ill? Is she really a Black Witch? Can she really enter his mind and make him ill? Are such things possible?

I personally don't doubt that they are possible, it's just that I have yet to meet anyone who is really able to do such things. Derren Brown creates a very good *illusion* of such things, but he doesn't claim any real psychic powers—he is very clear that what he does is "a mixture of "magic, misdirection, and showmanship."

Many schools of thought say that colluding with a delusion or reinforcing it is a very bad thing to do, and that arguing with them,

149

or correcting them, is a *good thing* to do. If you have ever tried arguing with a devout religious follower that his religion is wrong, you know that the chance that you will succeed in that is very close to zero.

So how do I help this guy? Change his belief? Reduce the hallucination? Challenge him?

I did none of those. I constructed him a powerful sigil—a charm or talisman—according to the instructions in The Greater Key of Solomon. He collected it a week later, and I gave him strict and detailed ritual instructions for its use. I didn't hear from him again for over a year, when I met him at a chance encounter during a business conference.

"I feel a bit awkward saying this," he told me in the queue for coffee, "but after I used the sigil in the way you described, I realised how silly I was being, and that there was no way that woman could be doing the things that I thought she was. But I didn't want to tell you, because I knew how sincere you were about the sigil and how it would work for me."

Magic can indeed be a strange art at times. Explained in Ericksonian terms, he was caught in a therapeutic double bind. The instructions were designed to act as a convincer for the efficiency of the sigil, but they also made him feel just a little bit silly. He'll either be convinced that he's now protected from malign psychic influence, or he'll realise that there isn't such a thing—a win-win situation.

When working with any particular problematic belief, I rarely see fit to challenge it. I know that it might seem counterintuitive to some people, but challenging a delusion can in fact actually make it stronger and tougher. So think of it in these terms—don't challenge it *or* reinforce it—instead, just accept it and *expand* it to make it more workable. To illustrate, I borrow a Zen story cited in Paul Reps' *Zen Flesh, Zen Bones*.

A young wife fell sick and was about to die. "I love you so much," she told her husband. "I do not want to leave you. Do not go from me to any other woman. If you do, I will return as a ghost and cause you endless trouble."

Soon the wife passed away. The husband respected her last wish for the first three months, but then he met another woman and fell in love with her. They became engaged to be married.

Immediately after the engagement, a ghost appeared every night to the man, blaming him for not keeping his promise. The ghost was clever, too. She told him exactly what had transpired between himself and his new sweetheart. Whenever he gave his fiancé a present, the ghost would describe it in detail. She would even repeat conversations, and it so annoyed the man that he could not sleep. Someone advised him to take his problem to a Zen master who lived close to the village. At length, in despair, the poor man went to him for help.

"Your former wife became a ghost and knows everything you do," commented the master. "Whatever you do or say, whatever you give your beloved, she knows. She must be a very wise ghost. Really, you should admire such a ghost. The next time she appears, bargain with her. Tell her she knows so much you can hide nothing from her, and that if she will answer you one question, you promise to break your engagement and remain single."

"What is the question I must ask her?" inquired the man.

The master replied, "Take a large handful of soy beans in your hand and ask her exactly how many beans you hold in your hand. If she cannot tell you, you will know that she is only a figment of your imagination and she will trouble you no longer."

The next night when the ghost appeared, the man flattered her, and told her that she knew everything.

"Indeed," replied the ghost, "and I know you went to see that Zen master today."

"And since you know so much," demanded the man, "tell me how many beans I hold in this hand."

There was no longer any ghost to answer the question. (37, pp. 57-58)

The Messiah Complex

"When I quit working, I lost all sense of identity
in about fifteen minutes."   —Paige Rense

The months approaching the new millennium saw a spate of messiahs preaching their own portents in badly-quoted biblical scripture. Almost inevitably, Jerusalem was clogged with enough messiahs for a special Field Psychiatric Task Force to be established in order to deal with what was to become known as "Jerusalem Syndrome"—mad messiahs flocking to Jerusalem because the two thousand year Second Coming was possibly several years overdue. (Modern scholars tell us that the Gregorian calendar may not be as accurate as previously believed.)

Of course, it has often been said that if Christ really did return, he'd probably just be locked up and madicated with all the other Christs, Judas' and Pontius Pilates on the wards. We can only wonder what Jesus would make of such treatment since his last visit to the planet didn't exactly end amicably. Maybe he'd *want* the Prozac and the safety of the sanatorium, if he saw the mess that resulted from his suggestion that we all actually start being nice to each other—people have had a nasty tendency to keep on killing other people in His name.

One interesting feature about the Messiah Complex is its prevalence amongst Christians when compared to other religions. We don't often come across a Mohammed or a Buddha in the street waving his arms and shouting frantically to "repent or die." I often wonder if this might be related to the fact that while *Jesus* was nailed to a cross, his impersonators tend to get a soft comfortable room, free food and drugs.

While Mohammed lived out the full life of the prophet, his impersonators run a grave risk of being chopped up for heresy before they ever get the chance to even smell the inside of that rubber room. If you are going to be a delusional impostor, you had better pick your target audience very carefully.

I guess this is where Richard Bandler's approach to such delusions comes in quite nicely. Rather than attempting to make the psychotic accept our reality (a fairly pointless waste of time) he suggests changing reality to fit the psychotic. Contrary to popular belief, the structure of psychosis is cohesive, tightly structured and usually *remarkably* stable. If external reality is made congruent with the psychotic realm, the psychotic immediately needs to change it. Think of it as a kind of polarity response; if the psychotic is rejecting reality, and you make reality fit his delusion, then he has to reject *that*. The real trick is to be able to directionalise this polarity shift to something that is more useful for the patient. So, when you are getting ready to hammer those nails into his warm soft hands, and he starts protesting that he isn't really Jesus, it's probably best to raise the tension just a little bit by shouting, "Hah! That's what the last one said!"

In a similar situation where the man-who-believed-he-was-a-corpse was being nailed into a coffin, in response to his frantic banging on the lid demanding that someone check his pulse again since he was really still alive, the therapist was heard to bellow, "Since when we did we ever let something like that spoil a good funeral?!" The patient's wife said that was the most animated she'd seen him in years.

It is often said that the most delusional patients are also the most paranoid. However, in my experience this isn't always quite true. For example, when I met a man who thought he was God (not just *a* god, but *the* God), he told me that he wasn't paranoid but rather that he was "just tired." I wasn't really surprised; the universe is quite a busy place with lots going on in it, so being God must be quite exhausting work.

"God" was one of my "budget clients"—I see several a week as my bit for the community, and they pay me any way they can. I was once paid with a big bag full of grapes—the client had no money, but he did have a very large grape vine in his garden. I brew my own wine; he had the grapes. So a deal was struck, the man changed and the wine brewed. Later on, one merry weekend I managed to change it back into water, too.

Slightly less satisfying, another client, a professional playwright, wrote me a play about a mad therapist. A local theatrical group performed it in a pub and the lead character kept waving him arms about. "Who's the lead guy based on?" I asked her. She didn't answer, she just raised her eyebrows.

"God" had agreed to pay me what he had in his pocket—which turned out to be exactly one pound in small change. I made a resolution at that point to think these things through a little more carefully in the future and asked him what he did for money. "Oh," he replied casually, "I'm claiming unemployment benefits."

Unemployment benefits! No wonder the world was in such a mess—God wasn't working! How long has this being going on? I asked, aghast.

"Since 1976, when I realised I was God." He said with a nod. This really was just too much; something had to be done. Either that, or I wanted a refund—or some decent wine.

The poor exhausted "God" lamented about how these days no one believed his story that he was God. I found this amazing—as I totally believed him. And I had no problem in breaking that little rule about not putting the Lord to the test—I demanded that he return my rabbit that was so cruelly taken from me as a child—a rabbit that really did end up on the dinner plate of my next-door neighbour.

They told me it was an accident, but I never really did buy that one. It was called Hoppity and I was 7 years old. Hoppity escaped and sat happily in the neighbour's garden, eating his vegetables. Freedom came at a huge cost to poor Hoppity, since being of similar appearance to every wild rabbit that had ever been in the vegetable patch before him, Hoppity got an air rifle pellet in the back of his head. On learning of his mistake the neighbour reportedly commented, "I did wonder why he sat so still before I shot him. So sorry."

I fell to my knees in front of "God" and prayed and prayed. I cried, I beseeched, I threw myself on his mercy. "God" desperately wanted to leave the office, but he couldn't, because I was clinging to his cloak pleading for a seat at his right hand. "Please, oh Lord, please! You and me for all eternity up there, pleeeease!" I think there was something about this last statement that made him a little uncomfortable. Maybe it was the way I kept waving my arms about when I spoke—one day I'll probably have someone's eye out.

I did detect just a little dent in his delusional structure, but he most definitely wasn't impressed. But after all, what did he *really* expect for a pound? Those little dents can add up. For example, one story tells of the female therapist who, when encountering a Mary Magdalene who was claiming, *"I'm fucking Jesus!"* dryly replied with a yawn, "I know, he told me about it last night." And there is the classic story of Milton Erickson who sent out the young institution-alised schizophrenic who claimed to be Jesus to go and help out the rednecks doing some remodelling on the hospital grounds, saying, "After all, you know about carpentry right?" This little dent just pro-vided a poke into the right direction. It doesn't take long to learn *not* to keep telling a redneck with a nail gun that his sins will be forgiven if only he'd "believe." Jesus, plus two planks of wood and a big scary redneck with a nailgun. The Romans would indeed be proud.

Whatever we choose to believe about the patient who claims to be the Messiah or any other biblical figure, it's worth considering just how the Mad Messiah will view *us*. The stiff psychiatrist may well be viewed with great pity, after all: "They know not what they do." Well, at least until the thorazine wipes out the ability to feel anything at all. Call it the psychiatrist's revenge. Stable delusional complexes don't really respond well to drugs, the patient just learns to stop mak-ing his claims in order to get the dosage reduced so that he can func-tion again.

I'd be interested to know exactly how my delusional clients view the few therapists willing to try out Bandler's approach—pos-sibly they view *us* as dangerous psychotics. The threat offered by such approaches is really only to the psychotic's delusional belief system, but the message is simple and always well received—I don't want you to *deny* your delusion, *I want your full conversion.* This is of course something every Mad Messiah already knows how to do. He's already done it once before; that's how he ended up in this pickle in the first place. Joe Bloggs converted to become the Mes-siah, and now we want Joe back again. So we just need to provide the right impetus and the right kind of direction. Heaven help us all.

Deletion

"I don't think there's anything unique about human intelligence. All the neurons in the brain that make up perceptions and emotions operate in a binary fashion." —Bill Gates

There is an old joke about the agoraphobics support group. You already know the answer—it failed because no one turned up. It's a bad joke; I'm just glad I didn't invent it. There are worse jokes of course, such as how does a badly-trained NLPer cure an agoraphobic from panic attacks? He gets the guy to think of pleasant things every time he feels bad. Not really a joke, just a poor use of sequential anchoring. These clients generally get to feel bad fairly frequently, so it isn't long before they start to feel bad about whatever used to make them feel good. You see, sometimes kinesthetic feelings linger longer than planned, With the negative kinesthetics running inside their neurology, the person may find that the things in life that used to be good now acquire the bad feeling.

Gregory Bateson posed an interesting question: "A certain mother habitually rewards her small son with ice-cream after he eats his spinach. What additional information would you need to be able to predict whether the child will:

a. come to love or hate spinach,

b. love or hate ice-cream, or

c. love or hate mother?"

It's a good puzzle indeed, and I have yet to come to a satisfactory conclusion.

Technology has enabled us to see what is occurring inside the brains of different categories of panickers. Whilst it is difficult to get the *agora*phobics to turn up for clinic appointments, functional brain scanning of *claustro*phobics is easy—just put them into the scanner tunnel and tell them to *try* to relax. The obsessives are even easier—just make the tunnel a bit dirty.

Now that we can see from various scanning methodologies the almost precise neurology of some behaviours, the neurosurgeons can literally burn out a pathway of obsession or compulsion. It is rumoured that operating departments often smell of frying bacon, but it is not breakfast that the casual visitor notices. However, that neural pathway that lights up on the functional MRI in anxiety is likely to have more than one function, and one of them is likely to be the ability to anticipate future events.

Computer owners are familiar with the following kind of notice: "Deleting this program may impact upon more than one program. Do you wish to continue?" This is possibly one of the few analogies to neurology taken from computers that actually works. Of course it would be nice if the warning message told you *which* programs might be impacted, but rarely do you find this out until you reboot. Except here we are talking hardware. Tapping your computer with a small hammer is not likely to remedy the software problem. It is likely to invalidate your warranty though. No refunds.

The strategies that people use can be effective in some contexts, ineffective in others, and in some others become just a plain pain in the arse. People naturally notice the latter, and their first response is typically that they want to just get rid of it; if you offered them a cheap lobotomy, many would accept. However, removing the strategy or interfering with it is not necessarily the best way forward. Doing so just might impact more than one area.

I'm reminded of one of Bandler and Grinder's clients in the early days who wanted to stop smoking. Since they were experimenting with hypnosis, they simply suggested that she forget that she had ever smoked in the first place. When she went home, her husband offered her a cigarette, and she said, "I don't want one of those things." He said, "Oh, you quit?" and she said, "I never smoked." He would show her a photograph with a cigarette in her hand and she would negatively hallucinate the cigarette, "There's no cigarette in my hand!" He would point to the nicotine stains on her fingers, and she would negatively hallucinate those as well. All this put quite a strain on their relationship. So they saw her again, restored her memory, and tried a more specific approach.

Unlike computers, many people don't even have the *first* warning about the possible effects of deleting a program, so it's important to consider the possible impact of your intervention. Even when a client *does* have a warning signal, it may be only a vague feeling of discomfort, or a little nonverbal twitch that the client may not notice. Then it is really imperative that the therapist *does* notice it, take steps to find out what other program might be impacted, and find a way to *adjust* the program rather than completely *delete* it.

During my first-ever hypnosis training, during one of the practice sessions, one of the students wanted to lose his fear of heights. He quickly proved to be an excellent hypnotic subject and was duly hypnotized and successfully lost his fear of heights. However, the following week he reported that he had been taking a significant numbers of risks. He had been provocative in bars with aggressive-looking guys, he had stopped worrying about busy traffic and would cross the road without looking and so forth. He had overgeneralized the change to all contexts, so that *all* his ability to experience fear was removed. "I feel just fine," he reported, "But I doubt I'll live long at this rate."

Slicing, dicing and cutting brains is generally seen as a bit brutal. By comparison, drugging a brain is seen as more positive and socially acceptable. We have SSRI's, neuroleptics, thymoleptics, anxiolytics, sedatives, stimulants, and an ever-expanding pseudo-alchemical blend of pharmaceutical concoctions designed for drugging a brain. Bathing synaptic junctions in a sea of chemical formulations, floating neurons on a wave of adjustment.

There are other bad ways of adjusting a brain of course, and NLP practitioners possess just a few of them. Twice now I've had worried phone calls from therapists who have embarked their phobic clients on a journey of double dissociation—dissociate, reverse movie, reintegrate, or some other variation on the theme. (1, ch. 7) Problems can occur when you perform such a task on the phobic who has a problem with vomiting. Fear of vomiting is remarkably common, and on the two occasions that these therapists called me they did the pattern too slowly. My guess is that vomit isn't a nice thing to swallow whilst running the movie in reverse. Bad programming indeed, but at least it's only the software.

Hubert The Hairless

*"Hair brings one's self-image into focus; it is vanity's proving ground.
Hair is terribly personal, a tangle of mysterious prejudices."*
—Shana Alexander

The problem with Hubert, who was a long-term agoraphobic, was that he didn't really *want* any change. Agoraphobia is a Greek word meaning "fear of the agora" or marketplace, and they weren't far wrong. Richard Bandler calls it a "rich person's illness," because if you are hungry and have to go out to work to earn a living, agoraphobia is impossible.

Like many full-time mental illnesses, I tend to think of it more as a career move. After all, why work for a living when you can stay at home all day instead and receive generous welfare payments? As an added bonus, after 11 months of continuously feeling bad, the payments increase, because it officially becomes a "disability." Stay at home and have people pay you. Food will arrive at your doorstep, and charities will give you a big television. The government will pay your rent.

Imagine explaining to an Eskimo that we pay people to stay at home for years on end and not come out. In addition, the *longer* they stay at home then the more money we give them—just as long as they say all the right things to the men in the white coats.

Hubert's problem began when he was 21. He lost his hair—a condition called "alopecia"—and he worried about what people said about him behind his back. He started staying in, never going out during the daytime. After all, people would surely laugh at his baldness. Even if they didn't do it out loud, they'd sure enough *think* it. People told him to wear a hat, but Hubert didn't like hats. After all, it was *everyone else* who was thinking negative things about him so why should *he* change?

159

After a while he was referred to a psychiatrist. Naturally Hubert didn't turn up. He couldn't of course—he didn't have any hair. After several missed appointments, (The shrinks obviously didn't get the joke!) Hubert received a visit from the "special" social worker. The shrink visits. A psychologist visits. A community psychiatric nurse visits. A medical student completing his thesis visits. Hubert told them all the same story about his hair. In turn *they* all told him to wear a hat. Interesting, but no one ever suggested wearing a toupee. My guess is that *everyone* knows that a man wearing a toupee will always look exactly like, well, like a man wearing a toupee—*always* funny.

The social worker organised the benefit payments, a washing machine, a television and a new carpet. The psychiatrist, aware that Hubert wouldn't wear a hat, prescribed an SSRI drug and some diazepam. But Hubert never filled the prescription because he couldn't go out to the drug store. Hubert knew that he couldn't go out because he didn't have any hair.

The psychologist decided some systematic desensitisation was in order. After the first session Hubert stopped answering the door. He didn't need to go outside just so the psychologist could ask how he felt about being outside. He already knew about that. Even *thinking* about going outside made him feel bad. On one occasion (failed visit #7 according to the notes) the psychologist tried to reason with Hubert through the letterbox that maybe some Cognitive Behavoural Therapy (CBT) would be of benefit. But Hubert correctly reasoned that no amount of CBT would ever replace his hair. Not knowing how to ask useful questions, the psychologist was at a loss for words, and not for the last time I'm sure. I wonder how he felt about that?

The medical student wanted to try some psychoanalysis to find the deep-rooted problem of Hubert's difficulty. Hubert stopped answering the door to him after the first session. "The only thing that is deep rooted," he told me, "is that I haven't got any hair."

I began to notice a pattern; maybe the problem was about Hubert's lack of hair. Or maybe it was about his mind-reading patterns. "You think I should wear a hat, don't you?" he said to me when we first met. "No." I replied, "I cannot think of a style that would suit you."

I didn't venture any further dialogue; I just cut the plug off the television set that was blasting away in the corner. *Anyone* who spends their day watching the drivel on daytime television really *really* needs to get out more often. Really.

Plug-cutting activities may not generate the kind of rapport that is so often emphasised in counselling training—"unconditional positive regard"—but they certainly shift the direction of focus. Given my attitudes, when I trained as a counsellor my trainer had to struggle very hard each week to maintain "unconditional positive regard" towards me. I certainly didn't make it easy for him, and it was clear that he simply didn't like me—there was something about his tone of voice and the little facial twitch he developed during the second week of the training. We were encouraged to bc "honest with our feelings" which sometimes turned out to be a little bit in conflict with "unconditional positive regard." *He* was being "unconditional," while *I* was being honest.

A peculiar phenomenon has been gaining momentum in Japan recently. If reports are to be believed, approximately one million young men have shut themselves in their rooms and they aren't coming out. Not ever. The phenomenon apparently began about 10 years ago and has been gaining popularity ever since. Young men, refusing to work or engage in social contact, lock themselves in their rooms and begin living in a twilight zone of solitude. One mother heroically said that from now on, in order to encourage her son to come out, she isn't going to slip an envelope containing his $400 monthly allowance under his door any more. In one remarkable case, one "shut in" cmerged just long enough to kidnap a 9-year-old girl in 1990 and kept her in his room until 1999. Nobody noticed. His mother who lived downstairs wasn't permitted to enter his room; I guess she wanted to respect his "personal space."

This phenomenon seems to have grown proportionally to the boom in their economy. Statistics prove many things, most of them quite untrue. But having a large number of agoraphobics in a culture does say something about its comparative wealth. Mumbai in India is seeing a similar problem with agoraphobics, and experts suggest it is related to anxiety. Having sat in a Mumbai traffic jam for 11 weeks, I can understand why. But more realistically it is probably related to the number of experts who are paid to observe such things. Where the economy is bad, there are no experts and no agoraphobics—they all starve to death or *have* to go out and get a proper job. It's a stark choice. Call it cultural homeostasis.

"But," I hear the analysts cry, "what about the root causes?" The root causes of hair loss or the root cause of culture? The microscope zooms downwards ever closer to it, and yet the diagnosis reflects a larger cultural bias. It isn't that the "agoraphobic" has to intentionally learn how to be a *proper* "agoraphobic," it's just that the diagnosis reflects what people are already thinking and doing within a cultural framework.

Whilst the Malaysians rampage with amok and the North Africans are possessed with bad spirits called "Zar," in southeast Asia there is "Koro," which is basically penis panic. The panic arises when the person believes that his penis is retracting into his body and that this will rapidly prove to be fatal. With its roots in Chinese cultural beliefs, it is thought that abnormal sexual practices may bring about a sufficient disturbance in the yin and yang balance that the vital energies are lost. Sometimes Koro is believed to occur as a result of witchcraft. These are all disorders that appear decidedly strange when seen from an alien cultural perspective, but does a fish know what it's like to be wet, I wonder?

So rather than peering down a microscope until we appear to be surveying the quantum level, how about zooming *out* to see the larger cultural picture? In order to do this, we have to change our own perspective first—not a popular activity amongst psychiatric professionals for sure. If they did step out of the diagnostic waters of the DSM-IVR diagnostic manual (18) they might begin to discover just how wet they actually are.

My intervention with Hubert took quite a long time to arrange— a little *too* long as it turned out. Gathering 100 bald men to converge and hold a conference on Hubert's new carpet was certainly not an easy task. It would have been a bit of a squeeze at best, but it might have yielded some interesting results. Part of the plan was to create a flotilla of baldness with Hubert sandwiched neatly in the middle as the bald armada set sail down the street. You can maybe see where I was leading with this idea. I had managed to gather exactly three willing volunteers when Hubert called and cancelled all further appointments. His social worker, a balding lady herself, had leaked my plan to Hubert and, unsurprisingly, he wasn't happy with it one little bit. I guess not everyone possesses the same sense of fun.

The social worker meanwhile wanted to arrange for a consultation with a trichologist to consider a hair transplant. I think maybe *she* was quite interested in it for herself. I suggested that a social worker transplant might be a better idea, but Hubert didn't want to argue with the lady who provided the new wide-screen television, clean carpets and his food deliveries. As one employer once told me: "If you are going to take *our* money then you play by *our* rules and do as *we* say." So I guess Hubert was just doing his job. He was moved shortly afterwards to a bigger flat with thicker walls to protect the neighbours from the excessive noise from the television.

When offered a bigger flat in a nicer neighbourhood, Hubert didn't seem to have much difficulty in going outside of his flat at all. I guess sometimes it's just a question of motivation. At this time I still lived in *The Bunker*, a tiny airless basement flat in the centre of Southampton, and as I gazed at the shapes in the ever-growing damp patch in the bathroom ceiling, I wondered if in fact maybe Hubert had made a good career choice after all.

Agoraphobia

"I claim that human mind or human society is not divided into watertight compartments called social, political and religious. All act and react upon one another." —Gandhi

Involuntary confinement without external stimulation or sufficient internal stimulation can drive someone insane pretty fast. However boredom doesn't appear to be much of a problem for an agoraphobic. When someone is hiding in fear, the fear seems to dramatically affect their perception of time. When the confinement is voluntary, and for a specific purpose—keeping that person safe—staying-in is a strategy to avoid a different and very real insanity.

Of the past 15 years, I have spent approximately three of them in India, divided among a number of trips. Whenever I go, I am usually booked up by clients very quickly, and tend to work pretty much in any setting. On my last trip, I ran group sessions out on the sandy beaches of northern Goa and functional neurology classes in a church the size of a large cathedral. It was fantastic and I will go back often.

In India the hospitality is second to none; in another's house, the guest is very much treated as a god. However, there is a price. In exchange, the guest is expected to act and behave with divine grace and manners at all times; for example, a proper guest *never* contradicts his host. This can lead to particular difficulties for mental health professionals when addressing issues such as the ever-increasing number of agoraphobics.

After a few weeks of patiently working through numerous issues possessed by my agoraphobic host, paying careful attention to the etiquette of Indian hospitality, I could take it no more. The net result of my being "honest with my feelings" landed me on the next overnight bus out of the city, where I was repeatedly groped by a computer programmer from Dubai.

I spent the next fortnight drinking cocktails and learning to boogie-board on the beaches of Goa, while my host sent furious emails around the world about my allegedly appalling conduct. On hearing about the situation, a Mumbai psychiatrist called to say, "You should *never* argue with an Indian agoraphobic, you just tell him to keep taking his medicine and wait until he either gets bored or he runs out of money." Possibly good advice indeed.

At this point I am reminded of the agoraphobic who was unable to go on any longer. He *knew* that to drive more than a mile from his house would result in an intense terminal fear that would surely kill him. So he started driving in a suicide attempt, and ended up in the beautiful countryside of Wales before he realised how far he had got—without any fear, and instead rather enjoying the country views. He was lucky. His suicide attempt didn't stop him living. And it did end the restricted lifestyle that had imprisoned him for more than 15 years.

In conversation with a colleague, I mentioned a client who measured her "comfort perimeter" around her house by street signposts. I went out in the car with her. She did something quite interesting. We got halfway down a particular road and she told me, "I cannot go past that sign post." The NLPer in me replied, "What would happen if you did?" "I see myself freaking out!" she said. So naturally, I got her to change those pictures of what she saw herself doing to something more useful.

At one seminar I gave regarding agoraphobia, a participant proposed installing a phobia about staying-in. While some may find such a view amusing, that would achieve little more than trapping the client between the proverbial rock and a frightening hard place, restricting their tiny and rigid worldview even more. Such approaches may indeed add a little entropy, but the client is not necessarily going to go in a useful direction, and any hope of success may well be left behind. NLP is about *adding* choices, not about taking them away.

In psychotherapy training, there is a lot of talk about "secondary gains" and of the importance of addressing these when embarking on any change work. But what about *primary* gains and the rules of social engagement? I might not be the most sociable guy on the planet, but even *I* know that in someone else's house you have to pay a little respect to *their* rules. If you don't, they can simply ask you to leave. If you don't leave, well, then there's probably a crime being committed.

As the rules of "therapy" become increasingly bureaucratic, and more and more lawyers approach people on the street seeking easy money at the cost of rationality, radical change work becomes increasingly difficult. Many of our civil laws only serve to encourage unhealthy behaviours and politically correct interventions such as mass madication and the financing of deviance.

There are drugs specifically prescribable for "agoraphobia," as though such behaviour resides solely in errant synaptic function. That approach makes as much sense as the old proposition that agoraphobia is caused by a faulty mitral valve in the heart or a viral infection. While a biological explanation may have some degree of merit, at most it is only a small piece in a very complex social phenomenon. To collectively scan the brains of agoraphobics in search of a neurological explanation makes as much sense as collectively scanning the brains of "koro" patients, or any other patient suffering from a culturally-bound pseudo-psychiatric condition. This is not to say that a collective scanning won't reveal some commonalities. I've often proposed scanning people by profession, such as comparing the similarities found among psychiatrists with the similarities found among, say, lawyers. Psychiatry a biologically deviant behaviour? You bet! But what about the lawyers?

NLP-oriented therapists are hopefully more conversant in cybernetics and systems theory than most traditional therapists. So I hope that they are more likely to be able to weave a pattern out of the complex social and legal rules that support a problem behaviour. Gathering information is vital, and attention to the larger context is crucial. A single session cure is not a likely possibility when dealing with agoraphobic behaviours, especially when we regard and challenge the extreme opinionation that appears to be common to so many long-term (predominantly male) agoraphobics. So go forearmed with Dilts' "sleight of mouth" language patterns (19) and don't expect a double dissociation phobia cure to do the job for you.

The reliance on techniques is the failing of so many therapists. They have a remarkable tendency to think in terms of diagnostic labels. "If we have the right diagnosis, then we can simply apply the right technique to the problem." That rationale leaves much to be desired—just because we can give the behaviour or symptom a name, doesn't mean we actually know anything about what is going on.

A Screaming Phobia

"I have this phobia: I don't like mirrors. And I don't watch myself
on television. If anything comes on, I make them shut it off,
or I leave the room." —Pamela Anderson

Several years ago a woman was brought in to me by a psychiatrist who was interested in observing how I work. She told me that the woman was suffering from a "pathological phobia of spiders." Now, I'm not entirely sure what a "pathological phobia" is, but I do know that none of the seventeen different psychiatric drugs this lady had been given had made it go away. Pathologically phobic or not, this lady was definitely a *screamer*. All I had to do was begin to hold out my right palm and she started shrieking blue murder. For some reason every arachnophobe assumes that the therapist is going to throw a spider at them. I think perhaps that this comes from the absurd process of "flooding," in which you either repeatedly expose the client to spiders, or simply lock the client in a room full of the buggers until, exhausted, they stop yelling.

As I said, this lady was a true screamer, which wasn't really surprising. When I asked her about how the spider in my hand would look, she described—in between hyperventilated terror—a moving image of a spider that was about 60 feet high, three-dimensional, in full-focused Technicolor, with full sound effects. Imagine hearing the sounds that a 60-foot spider might make! I quickly hypnotised the psychiatrist and gave her the suggestion that a small spider would sit comfortably and peacefully in the palm of her outstretched hand.

Then, I turned my attention back to the client, who was now intently focused on the psychiatrist's palm, and as a result indirectly in a light trance. I told her to slightly enlarge her image before beginning to shrink it down *only at the same rate and speed that the spider in the hand of the psychiatrist began to grow uncontrollably.* It was a neat trick, and I wasn't entirely sure that that I could pull it off, but at that time I was still addicted to the "act as if" frame which made me wonderfully annoying to the few friends who had survived my earlier experimentations.

What I was hoping for was to transfer the phobia to the psychiatrist, to develop a little empathy for her client. Of course that wouldn't really be complete unless we could drug her too. However, what actually happened was that the client did indeed reduce down her image and calmed down appreciably. But interestingly she became afraid of the *psychiatrist*, which I wasn't expecting at all. The psychiatrist on the other hand did not have any change in her representation of the spider—maybe my indirect suggestion was a little *too* indirect. She told me afterwards this was because she could in no way imagine the client ever being able to do anything that would reduce her fear. The psychiatrist truly believed that the client could never change—while collecting weekly fees for trying to help her change.

It was only in the imagination of the client that the psychiatrist's spider got larger. The client said afterwards, "I didn't want it to get too big in case it scared her, so my spider didn't really get all that small, but it's much better now." The client left with a full working knowledge of the NLP phobia cure. But despite observing a first-hand "up close and personal" demonstration, the psychiatrist left as clueless as when she arrived.

"Allergy"

A number of years ago when I was still a casualty nurse, I was on duty with the resuscitation team when a man arrived "under a blue light" and police escort. He was suffering a severe anaphylactic reaction. Anaphylaxis is a catastrophic allergic reaction, which if left untreated can often be rapidly fatal.

Our patient had been working outdoors in a labouring gang and had apparently been bitten on the lower leg by an adder (viper) snake, a rare species in the UK. His symptoms were unmistakable—his face was heavily swollen, particularly his lips, tongue and eyelids, his blood pressure had plummeted, his skin had hives and a heavily mottled appearance, his breathing was laboured and greatly distressed.

I began removing all the patient's heavy work clothes whilst some of the team worked rapidly to get the guy stabilised. High-flow oxygen was supplied, intravenous access was acquired, life-saving fluids were given, and the drugs adrenaline and chlorphenaramine were administered.

Yet whilst all this was going on, one unmistakable detail became quite apparent. The bite was apparently to the lower left leg but the crew had been unable to locate the exact position of the bite. Their main concern had been keeping him stable and transferring him as quickly as possible to the emergency department.

Despite the heat of the day, this man had been wearing knee-high Doctor Martin boots and fairly hefty combat trousers—essentially, there was *no way* that he could have been bitten by a snake. A snake *had* bitten *at* him (it was witnessed by others) and probably made contact with the boot, but there was no possibility that this creature had injected any venom into him. Toxicology later confirmed this. Yet this man was clearly experiencing a near-fatal allergic reaction.

Subsequent follow-up demonstrated that he had never experienced a severe allergic reaction before, which ruled out any reference experience. If he'd had one, it would have been possible for it to be triggered by the "suggestion" of the bite. Later allergy tests demonstrated only a mild response to certain pollens—common hay fever. Now, to help connect some dots. . . .

Anaphylaxis, like many emotional responses, is *learned*. It is rare to have a serious allergic reaction upon the first exposure to a substance, but the severity of the reaction can increase exponentially with repeated exposure. This makes our snake man a bit of a medical mystery, and I've always liked medical mysteries because they show that we don't really know everything. Furthermore, exploring such anomalies often reveal new and different ways of thinking about things.

More recently I have been working with a man who was employed at a sawmill workshop for the majority of his adult life— some thirty years. Inevitably, despite correct health and safety procedures, there is always a certain level of wood dust present in the workshop environment.

One day last year he started to become unwell, but with a strong work ethic and a tendency to consider all doctors "quacks" he ignored the illness and struggled on. He laboured on for about 16 days before collapsing at work, when he was taken to hospital and diagnosed with severe pneumonia. Overnight his condition worsened and a weeklong stay in intensive care followed. His convalescence was lengthy, and it took several months for him to be able to climb stairs comfortably without becoming short of breath and turning a rather alarming shade of blue.

During those 16 days of severe *physiological* stress due to his pneumonia, this man was exposed to the wood dust in the workshop. As a result, his immune system had connected the stress response from pneumonia to the *dust*, and now he has acquired a severe and dangerous reaction upon exposure to wood dust. He has seen a doctor and been told that he has a "condition." The condition is called, "asthma," and of course the solution is medication.

An allergy is a sort of phobia of the immune system. The immune system mounts an intense response due to some stress or challenge, and connects this response to a harmless substance. When the specific trigger for an allergic response is known, there is a simple method for eliminating it. (1, ch. 5) However, that method works best when the allergen is known, and it's difficult to use when the client is already responding to the allergen at the time of treatment.

I've seen something similar with fear. One child stood in front of the class confidently one day for show-and-tell and was laughed at and humiliated by the other children. Weeks later, he is expected to present in front of the class again, but that morning he feels "unwell" and his mum keeps him home from school. As an adult, he avoids public presenting wherever possible, and when he can't avoid it, he feels like a nervous child and leaves the stage feeling like a failure. His anxiety generalises to other contexts in his life, and before long his avoidance behaviours also increase. His stomachaches and headaches and his skin rashes and muscle twitches continue, his sleep suffers, and his health is often poor. He sees his doctor who tells him he has a "condition." The condition is called, "generalized anxiety disorder," and again the solution is medication.

I'm told that the only two naturally built-in fear responses in an infant are of falling and of loud noises; all others are learned. Show a small child a snake for the first time, and he will not be afraid. But if you show him the snake and then startle him with a loud noise, he will associate the startle response to the snake and will become phobic of snakes. This was dramatically demonstrated almost a hundred years ago by psychologist John Watson with his "Little Albert" experiment—one that defied all ethical thinking—in which the very young Albert was exposed to furry animals which he liked, until Watson started making frightening clanging noises which startled the unfortunate Albert. It wasn't long before the furry animals triggered the fear response and generalised to all furry things, including Albert's favourite teddy bear.

Simple phobias such as this are common and can be induced in many ways. A child is playing with an unfamiliar dog, the dog suddenly reacts to something and turns nasty, and the child is bitten and frightened. The child learns to avoid dogs to avoid being bitten again. Someone else has the unfortunate experience of a wasp flying inside their clothing and buzzing around furiously before stinging them as they frantically try to remove it. Exposure to another wasp later on triggers the fear response—and perhaps an allergic response as well—as the body primes its immune system to combat the allergen.

A simple phobia of this kind is a conditioned response that can be *re*-conditioned just as easily, and it tends to respond well to the traditional NLP "fast phobia cure." (1, ch. 7) But what about phobias which do not respond to this technique? I have seen dozens of clients who have tried in vain many times to overcome their phobia, and have seen many different NLP practitioners and hypnotherapists, but continue to have their fear response.

These more resilient and disabling phobias tend to lack any direct personal experience of the phobic object. What the phobic person has experienced is exposure to *someone else's* phobic reaction to the object. For example, recently a friend visited my home along with her 2-year-old son. She made the mistake of interpreting the cute little noises of Minky, one of my pet rats, as an invitation to put her finger through the bars of the cage. Minky is a fearless creature, who will readily attack the vacuum cleaner and who used to launch spectacular assaults on the washing machine. He can mutilate a fingertip with impressive ferocity and astonishing speed.

The 2-year-old missed the exact details of what had occurred. What wasn't missed was his mother's rapid withdrawal from the cage and accompanying shrieks and cascade of vernacular that poured forth at great volume. To the 2-year-old, witnessing mother have such a reaction after approaching the cage in the corner was enough of a message to stay away from that part of the room, no matter how much reassurance was offered—as a result of single learning experience. (On the rat cage there is now a sign that says, "We Eat People. We do.")

But what if the mother already has, or develops, a phobia of some sort and regularly displays behaviours that clearly signal to the child both the mother's fear and distress and her beliefs about the object? The child may never be directly exposed to the object, but when he is, these *beliefs* that the child has developed about the object will come into action. It is these beliefs that maintain the emotionally catastrophic reaction that does not respond to the fast phobia cure.

I had a nice confirmation of this from a colleague who worked with a man who had a phobia of bees. This client had a somewhat paranoid belief that bees would intentionally seek him out to sting him. Here is the colleague's report:

"I had trapped a few bees—and having been a beekeeper, I knew that after a little time away from the hive, bees become very disorganized and very unlikely to sting, *and* when released in a room will always fly toward the light to try to escape. After telling him all this, I got his permission to let ONE bee out of the jar. He was very tense, but the bee flew directly to the window, rather than attacking him, in contrast to his belief that they would seek him out. The "tipping point" for him was when he realized that his phobia of bees was like his father's more extensive fears—and he *really* didn't want to be like his father! Then I opened the jar and inverted the opening over my hand and waited until one landed on my hand and walked around on it without stinging. After some talk, he agreed to do the same. Initially very tense, he gradually relaxed, with a look of total amazement on his face. Later we tested his response by taking him to a bee yard, where he approached the hives with bees flying all around—initially with a bee hat and veil, and then without it. He saw me without a bee hat, and thought to himself 'He doesn't need a bee hat; I don't need a bee hat.' The next night he had a dream in which bees were in his bed and he was completely comfortable with them—as if they were just little cozy teddy bears. Follow-up five years later confirmed that he was still pleased with the change. Every time he is near a bee, he is delighted all over again to no longer have the 'knee-jerk' response of fear and avoidance."

Fairy tales and other strange stories we tell children can develop these beliefs well. As a child, the most frightening thing I could imagine was being lost in the woods at night, because of all the monsters and bad things that I had grown to believe lived in there. As we got older, the neighbourhood kids started daring each other to go farther and farther into the woods at night, so step-by-step we learned to confront and nullify that particular set of beliefs. This method, called "systematic desensitization," does work, but it is glacially slow.

I wonder if our snake man, mentioned earlier, had seen other people's reaction to snakes? He'd never been bitten by a snake before, but maybe his body did already know what to do. He was of a similar age to me, and I grew up on a Saturday afternoon television diet of cowboy movies where the lesser heroes were regularly either killed by an "Indian" or bitten by a snake. I never actually encountered a real snake until I was about 26, but as I child I was *very* familiar with what rattlesnakes could do, and the (now disproved) method of saving the victim's life with the "cut, suck and spit" method. (When playing in the woods, we carried our little penknives at all times, just in case.)

One seriously phobic client who had borne witness to many NLP practitioners' failings suffered an extreme phobic reaction to needles and injections. She had no recollection of ever actually receiving an injection or anything like it, yet had always been profoundly phobic. Even saying the word, "injection" would trigger a flinch response. Her fear was so overwhelming that even seeing something connected with injections on the television would cause her to feel very unwell, and she would often faint. She demonstrated this quite unwittingly as she sat down and attempted to describe her problem to me. Her eyes started rolling about as the colour drained from her face and she started flailing her arms about as she collapsed right in front of me in a dead faint on the floor.

As she came round looking rather nauseous, I said, "Wow! Can you do that again?" That wasn't quite the response she was used to; usually a therapist confronted with something so unexpected and dramatic began to panic a little, thus reinforcing her response.

"Every therapist I've seen before has said that this is the most serious phobia they have ever seen," she told me. The funny thing is that I hear this rather a lot from my clients. Whilst she was still on the floor I looked directly into her eyes, changing my own focus to makes things a little blurry and asked her, "Do you know what an injection actually *is*?" She flinched momentarily, and then she looked blank. Thinking about this for a moment, she admitted that actually she'd never really thought about it before.

I kept my stare fixed on her eyes and said, "I believe you." And then in a dull, monotonous voice I proceeded to quote boring academic details out of a medical procedures manual that I had borrowed from a nursing colleague. I gave the guidelines regarding technique, safety, regulations and correct "sharps" disposal, and I went on and on. Most people would have either interrupted me or displayed signs of boredom as I continued, but she listened attentively.

As I came to an end, I informed her in the same monotonous tone of voice that positioned at the back of the room on the table by the rat cage was a medical bag. I told her that in the bag was a large assortment of injection equipment and that if her curiosity was sufficiently raised she might care to open it. I assured her that at no point would I touch any of the things, and it was entirely her decision to go and have a look. She hesitated for only a moment before getting up off the floor and opening the bag and taking out the assortment of needles and syringes that were still in their sterile packaging.

I really didn't need to do or say much else. The look of wonder on this woman's face said enough. It was as though she was a small child, and was unlocking the greatest mystery of all. As she continued to handle the packets and began to open them up, I wondered what on earth her previous therapists had been doing? If they had been using the "double dissociation" technique, without a reference experience I couldn't help but wonder just what exactly they would have been dissociating her from? It seemed obvious to me that what was needed was to build a *associated positive* reference experience rather than dissociating her from a bad one. This woman had had a profound fear response, yet she didn't really know what she was afraid of.

"Can I put them together?" she asked me, with a syringe and needle now both out of their packaging. I didn't answer the question and just looked at her without offering any clue or direction. "Oh, I guess I can," she said as she put the two pieces together before opening up all the other packets and putting the pieces together.

In the medical bag was also an orange, some ampoules of normal saline, a sharps disposal bin and the guidelines for practicing injection techniques given to student nurses. For some reason, student nurses are told to practice injections on oranges; I guess it is traditional or something.

"Can I try injecting the orange?" she asked, but again I gave no hint of a clue as to direction. She studied the instruction sheet closely before drawing up the saline from the ampoule and gently injecting the orange. The entire time that childlike look of wonder never left her face.

She laughed and said she'd never realised how simple injections were. She tried out different sizes of needles—the smaller gauge needles need firmer and slower pressure owing to the increased resistance—and different sized syringes and soon needed a second and then a third orange. Soon she had run out of needles and said simply, "I think I am cured," something of an understatement.

The following day she telephoned me in excitement. The blood test that she had been avoiding but which was required for a genetic health screen had been carried out without a problem. "It wasn't exactly nice, but you know, it was nothing like I had ever feared it would be. I am cured."

Early Beginnings

"A ship in harbour is safe, but that is not what ships are built for."
—William Shedd

Like many therapists, my clinical work started by accident. I wanted to learn hypnosis, but didn't have any money. So knowing nothing about it whatsoever, I put an advert into the local newspaper: "Southampton Experimental Hypnosis Group starts this week." I expected one or two people to turn up. But on the first evening, *sixty-five* expectant people turned up. I was terrified, and had no idea what to do, but I was also very excited. I knew that this was the beginning of *something*. Quite what it was the beginning of, I am still finding out.

About a year passed before a medical student came along clutching a copy of *Frogs into Princes*. (9) I'd never heard of Bandler or Grinder, and I devoured every word in that book with relish. At this point I had started formal training in Ericksonian Hypnosis. On taking the course, I initially thought this was Erik, the psychiatrist. I'd never heard of the name Milton. My first thought was, "What a weird name—it must be made up or something."

I clearly had a lot to learn, and began practicing hypnosis at every opportunity. I worked at a hospital in the big emergency department at the time, so I had a lot of surprisingly willing staff and colleagues to practice on. Before long, I had people from other departments asking for a session, as they'd heard about the things that I was doing. Initially people complained of common problems, such as a desire to lose weight or stop smoking. Soon calls were coming in regarding insomnia, anxiety, stress and depression. My interest in psychiatry was also well-known, and before long my work went professional as I spent more and more time with patients and their families lost deep inside the psychiatric system.

This work has led me into various unfamiliar realms. Once I was invited onto local radio to take part in a debate about psychiatry—where I found myself overwhelmed with unexpected public speaking anxiety! I quickly learned that my views were possibly too controversial for a small local radio station, and I was rapidly ushered out of the studio as they cut to the commercial.

Later a daytime TV show invited me on to take part in a live studio discussion on the treatment of schizophrenia. I foresaw a probable set-up where I'd be torn to pieces by an audience of mostly emotionally-charged pro-psychiatric families of schizophrenics, so I turned it down. Sometimes issues regarding mental health are not open to sense and logic. I learned long ago that TV shows are seldom about information—more often they are about entertainment—in much the same way as throwing political and religious outcasts to the lions used to be in distant times.

Psychiatric care in general often seems to be lacking in humour, and where humour is absent, the void is often filled by despair. Working in mental health facilities I introduce a sense of comedic anarchy in order to bring about a systemic change that doesn't rely on pharmaceutical corporations to produce ever more potent psychotropic medications. This has often proven very unpopular with psychiatric colleagues. I have been dismissed from employment on a number of occasions, and have often been told that despite my high popularity with psychiatric patients, I simply don't take mental "illness" seriously enough to "cut it" in psychiatry.

Painting The Dog

"A three year old child is a being who gets almost as much fun out of a fifty-six dollar set of swings as she does out of finding a small green worm."   —Bill Vaughn

In August, 1994 I put a handwritten notice on a hospital notice board: "Student Hypnotist seeks Human Guinea Pigs for Hypnosis Experiments. No Insurance. Your safety is not guaranteed."

I was just 26 days into the Ericksonian hypnosis course and needed experience. I didn't expect to receive many phone calls from the advertisement, but I was sure I would get at least a few. Instead I received a steady stream of calls, maybe 15-20 a week for the next month or two and this was more than enough to get me started.

So I quit work for a while and started booking people in. I tried *everything*—rapid inductions, slow inductions, funny inductions, and even *no* inductions. Some poor souls I'd invite over, sit them down and then talk about anything and everything that *wasn't* hypnosis. When the hour was up, I'd thank them, shake their hand and send them on their way. I just wanted to see what would happen. A week after their session, I sent out questionnaires to everyone to ask for their opinions and experiences. This was useful feedback and curiously some of those on the receiving end of non-inductions reported interesting experiences as though they had been hypnotised quite deeply.

Other feedback gave me valuable pointers regarding my own behaviours:

"You spoke too quickly."

"I needed to use the toilet, but I felt too embarrassed to say anything, which is why I couldn't concentrate."

"I thought you were too young to be a decent hypnotist."

"I expected an old man with a beard and a limp."

"You sounded too much like a salesman."

"You weren't wearing any shoes."

I started asking people a simple question—"If hypnosis could do just one thing for you, what would you like that thing to be?" Because of the location of my advertisement, most of my guinea pigs were medical or nursing students, and their answers all seemed to have common themes:

1. To be happier.
2. To be more popular.
3. To have more money.
4. To have more frequent/better sex.

My Gran used to say that it is the simple things in life that makes us the happiest. This is so often true. For example, when I regressed one man back to "the happiest moment in your life so far," he dissolved into utter delight and started speaking as though he were a very young child.

"How old are you?" I asked.

"Six," he said, giggling and jiggling around.

"And what are you doing?" I asked.

"Painting the dog!" He replied gleefully. Apparently he'd found a tin of blue gloss paint in the garage. He'd had a lovely time, but his mother was horrified—she had to clean up the mess and shave the dog.

A Fractured Penis

*"I find that most sensitive issues are best dealt with
by using no sensitivity whatsoever."*
—Andrew T. Austin, showing his sensitivity.

The first time I encountered a fractured penis was while working in the Accident and Emergency department. A guy came sprint-
ing across the parking lot like a frightened gazelle, and into the
department faster than anyone we had ever seen. The sprinters always
presented something that would provide a story to tell the following
shift. We knew before he even made it to the door that this was going
to be something pretty interesting, if not eye-watering.

The previous record holder was a cricketer who had brilliantly
managed to deflect a ball with his thumb, resulting in the thumb tele-
scoping midway up his wrist. *That* guy could really move, I tell you.
Getting him to sit still long enough to inhale the Entonox was a mission in itself, and left us all wondering about the policy for giving
pain-relieving gas to a patient who is jumping up and down yelling,
"It hurts, it really fucking hurts!"

This situation was solved by a burly sister nicknamed "Shot Put
Helga" shouting, "Sit DOWN, *SHUT UP* and breathe on *THIS!*" while
stuffing the Entonox mask firmly onto his face. I guess sometimes you
just have to be direct in order to provide sufficient and effective relief.

Patients often get things totally wrong, and many will tend to
catastrophise to amazing degrees, mentally turning a small ailment
into something disastrous and life-threatening. One couple, out cel-
ebrating at a wedding the previous evening, brought themselves in
with the belief that their rather severe hangovers were symptoms of
terminal meningitis.

Media scares often bring in large numbers of worried citizens
seeking reassurance and advise. One tabloid hack managed to get a

181

major misunderstanding into print in the "Cats get AIDS" story that ran in the media for a few days after the "Gay Plague" hysteria had died down and the tabloids desperately searched for the latest scare story. For weeks afterward it seemed that every cat owner who had ever been bitten or scratched came in for AIDS testing, and would refuse to be reassured until they'd been jabbed with a needle at least once. It was a bit like what we termed "therapeutic x-rays." Because ankle sprains can swell to a frightening size and go through a striking range of colours, if it isn't x-rayed, the patient will continue to worry that in fact their ankle *is* broken. So they return again and again until they get that x-ray. People with ankle sprains recover far more quickly if they receive an x-ray than if they don't. People just love technology.

Now, I'd never even *heard* of a fractured penis, so to be encountered by a man screaming, "I have fractured my *penis*!" was a bit of a surprise. So you can understand that my natural reaction, as the caring sympathetic nurse who deals with the uninformed public on a daily basis, was to suggest that he calm down a bit.

He grabbed hold of my ears and shouted, "LISTEN YOU BASTARD! *I HAVE FRACTURED MY PENIS!* Now *do* something!!" Suddenly it was all very clear. With a frightened and aggressive man holding onto my ears, I figured a good plan would be to agree with him.

Now, for those as clueless as I was about such matters, here's how it happens. First, let's begin with a little anatomy—the penis is constructed so that blood flows into spongy sacs that fill with blood under high pressure to create an erection (a whopping 100 pounds per square inch in dogs, compared to a mere 4-16 in humans). When the blood leaves, it leaves though vessels on the outside of these sacs.

Now, the annals of emergency surgery reveal that more than one wrench has had to be removed surgically following its use as an erection aid. Think about it—blood flows in until a critical pressure is reached, closing the vessels that enable the blood to leave by compressing them against the spanner. This is bad. I personally have known surgeons who have amputated more than one penis owing to the delay between the "Oh shit!" phase turning to the "Uh ohhh" phase. There's the guy, with a spanner on his dick haplessly waiting (as his penis turns black) for desperation to overcome the embarrassment of the situation and the fear of being laughed at. In such dilemmas there is only one realistic choice: suffer the embarrassment and save the penis. I find it amazing how often people do the opposite. I guess shame and embarrassment really do have quite a crippling effect on an effective decision strategy.

Most emergency staff can tell you of at least one occasion where they were involved in removing a foreign body from an orifice where such foreign body was never meant to be put. The one I found the most curious was the guy with an apple in his rectum. He'd spent most of the day trying to expel the fruit but without success. He sensibly realised it was probably best to wait no longer and go get competent help. What creates the smirks on the faces of the staff is not so much that they are treating a guy with something unusual in his bottom; it's rather in response to the explanations that so often go with it. Now OK, I am sure that at least once in modern history someone has been digging in the vegetable patch naked and fallen over backwards onto a critically angled cucumber, or was vacuuming in the nude when incredibly their penis got sucked into the vacuum pipe. These stories permeate emergency folklore on a regular basis—we've heard them all many times over. So when told an explanation about how as the guy was unloading the groceries in the nude, he slipped and that was how the tin of baked beans got there, it can be very hard to keep a straight face.

But back to the anatomy of the penis. (The squeamish may wish to look away for a moment, and skip to the next paragraph.) On erection, these sacs fill with blood and maintain quite a high pressure—hence the rigidity. Apply sufficient force, say from the downward bounce of a female pelvis at a critical angle, and the thing can quite literally snap in half, bursting those sacs, which then expel the blood under great force into the surrounding tissues. In turn, the skin containing this calamity can also rupture, which as you might care to imagine isn't at all good, constituting a somewhat disturbing, messy, and very serious surgical emergency.

Hence, our man of the moment was whisked off to the operating department rapidly for expert surgery and his sexual future was thus assured.

With this little bit of knowledge in mind, it was several years later that I found myself in the company of a man who had already exhausted several counsellors and psychiatric professionals in an attempt to find help with his intractable and unremitting depression. When he arrived he looked awful; he was visibly in a very bad way.

"So, how did this all begin?" I asked this deeply unhappy man who didn't just weep—he blubbed and blubbed and threatened my new office chair with copious amounts of snot.

"It all started when I fractured my penis," he said as he broke into even louder sobs. I was half expecting him to add, "and I went to the hospital and had to contend with an idiot who didn't believe such a thing was possible," but he didn't. Thankfully, this was a different guy.

"I knew it was *really* serious when it burst! I thought I was going to bleed to death. My wife ran next door to get the neighbours for help. They called an ambulance and then they came over too— bringing the other neighbours with them."

By the time the ambulance had arrived, a large crowd had gathered and were all collectively starting to learn—first hand—just exactly what a burst penis entails. He was wheeled out through the crowd of shocked and newly-enlightened neighbours.

Obviously the man had survived, but unfortunately in his neighbourhood he was always going to be known as the man whose penis burst during that stormy night in '86. He was also a man so terrified of having sex again that he'd taken to sleeping in the spare room.

The problems grew. Months after surgery the scar lines began to contract, causing a significant bend to his organ that required further surgery to straighten things out again.

Even *thinking* of an erection or sex was enough to cause this man traumatic flashbacks, shame, and embarrassment. Hearing any innuendo or joke about sex did the same, and in these modern times these are absolutely everywhere and very hard to escape. This definitely wasn't good.

So it was no wonder he was depressed; he must have had an awful lot of flashbacks in the 15 years since the awful event. And while his wife was fairly sympathetic, after all those years she was beginning to miss out on sex somewhat.

"What if it bursts again?" he asked me as he completed his story.

"*What if?*" those two words that cause so much misery and anxiety in this world. When you hear those words as a therapist, you can offer as much reassurance as you like, apply as much logic and as much reasoning as you can muster, but the structure of "What if?" and the strikingly vivid images that follow those words, are likely to defeat you. Much like Sinbad slaying his demons; as soon as you squash one of them, two more pop up in its place. So, *"What if* it bursts again" is the point that so far no counsellor, group therapy, or industrial strength SSRI or anxiolytic drug had yet managed to move the man beyond. He looked up tearfully at me in expectation of an answer, some reassurance, or maybe hope.

"If it *does* burst again, could you take a photo?" I asked innocently.

"What?!" he said with more than a little surprise.

"A photo—you see these things don't happen very often, so us medical professionals don't really ever get to see what they look like fresh. So how about it?" I fixed my gaze on his eyes and raised my eyebrows—the universal signal for the other person to speak. But he couldn't—he was in a state of abject confusion, trying to work out if I was serious.

So, a quick explanation here. This guy has a movie in his mind of the horrible event playing over and over in an endless loop. He is also associated *into* the movie as though it is happening again. These two features are almost universal in such flashbacks, especially the bad ones associated with post-traumatic stress disorder (PTSD). The trigger for the replay of the movie is anything related to sex, or any sexual reference. Despite repeated exposure to all these stressors and triggers, no desensitisation had occurred—in fact he went on to develop further emotionally traumatic complications in consequence of the bend in his penis that had required further surgery.

I'm going to assume the reader is familiar with the NLP double-dissociation cure for PTSD that changes the reference experience for most phobias and traumas. (p. 209) A photo is a *still* picture, and imagining any event through the eye of a camera lens also distances the experience in other ways, separating the viewer from what is viewed. A photo is *framed* or *bordered*, and *two-dimensional*, making it much harder to associate into it. (Not many photos are 3-D yet.)

There are so many camcorder freaks that never get to enjoy any fun experience because they are so busy videoing it for later. I know, because I see them whenever I go on holiday. So "Can you take a photo" is a suggestion that is totally unexpected, initiating a desperate search for meaning. It is also a suggestion for a *still* picture with a degree of dissociation.

But notice—I've also snuck in there, "You see these things don't happen very often" *without* it being inside the frame of "reassurance." I've also validated his point of view with "Us medical professionals don't really ever get to see what they look like fresh," indicating that us medical professionals don't see it the same way that he does.

So, with presuppositions loaded and launched, I sat there maintaining my look of innocence. As you can probably imagine, I had *many* opportunities to practice this well as a child—with my eyebrows raised, watching as his face went through a somersault of emotional expressions, finally landing on laughter.

"Oh my God!" he said laughing, "You *are* serious!'

"Too damned right!" I continued on, "You have the most dysfunctional penis I have ever met." I raised my eyebrows again. Keeping them raised, I added, "Your wife must *still* be in shock—'gave him such an orgasm, his penis burst!'—poor cow, would be enough to put any *normal* woman off sex for life!"

Notice the contradiction here. According to his story, his wife *is* still interested in sex; this is an integral part of the presenting problem. And it wasn't an orgasm that burst his penis. But most important, I have shifted his attention away from *him* and introduced his *wife's* perspective into the equation.

"Just imagine how the neighbours must see *her* these days!" This shifts his attention even further to the neighbors' point of view. He just *has* to disagree with this one—or so I thought.

"You are right, but my wife isn't normal—she's been amazingly supportive of me." But I refused to take the bait to go back into his "poor me" frame.

"Stuck by *you* for sure, but that dysfunctional *penis* of yours. . . .?" I let the sentence trail off, leaving the implication hanging in the air. Eyebrows raised again, I drop the angle of my head and fix a stare.

His brain did more somersaults in order to process this. Only a few seconds earlier he was sobbing and stuck inside the movie of that fateful night. But now he's moved out of that—first into laughter, then to his wife's and then his neighbors' points of view, and now he is being hit with the suggestion that his wife has deserted his dysfunctional penis for someone else's.

He started laughing again, mouthing, "Oh my God. Oh my God" several times under his breath.

And in the style of the legendary Frank Farrelly, I asked in all innocence, "So, what's the *problem?*" as if nothing that has been said so far has been a problem.

Now having seen Farrelly working with clients, a common reaction to his style of working is a kind of "concussion" where the client struggles to make sense of reality and has to determine exactly *which* reality they are in.

This guy simply muttered something along the lines of, "God! I've been so stupid!" To which I could only reply, "You have only *just* noticed?" which elicited yet more laughter.

So there you have it. Within minutes of meeting a guy who had been too scared to make love to his wife for 15 years, a man who experienced intense traumatic flashbacks to a highly personal and potentially serious accident, we had achieved a profound shift in belief and attitude. But we weren't entirely finished.

"Forget the photo," I said. "Take a video camera; there are quite a few people who need you to do this."

He looked at me, confused, but smiling—waiting for what was coming next.

"I'll bet there hasn't been a pregnancy in your neighbourhood for over 15 years! Those poor neighbours need *someone* to let them know it's safe for sex again!"

By suggesting, "Forget the photo," I am giving a suggestion for amnesia of the movie-to-photo shift suggested earlier (which involved a possible repetition of that fateful night).

"Take a video camera" elicits a *new movie* of sexual activity, and it is also a mental rehearsal of this future activity. "There hasn't been a pregnancy in your neighbourhood for over 15 years!" is a reframe of the neighbours' reaction. "Those poor neighbours" aren't laughing at our man—they have also been frightened into celibacy. Now they are described as *participants* in the trauma, rather than voyeurs—and it also enables me to deliver the suggestion, "it's safe for sex again," while keeping our man at the centre of the story; he is the *someone* to enable this good deed to occur.

Follow-up six weeks later determined that things had indeed been very different. His manner was happier, more confident and lively. He really did look 10 years younger than he had previously, and he had a good colour to his face. "We have been making up for lost time," he said with a wink.

Illumination

"Lighten up, will you?"
—Request from Heroic Howard to Serious George on Ward B.

Brightness is a submodality that is often revealed in someone's language, often expressing the degree of someone's intelligence, understanding, or enthusiasm.

"That's a bright idea."

"You brighten up my life."

"The future looks bright."

"I have only a dim understanding of that."

"He's really enlightened."

"He's always keeping me in the dark."

"She's got a dazzling career ahead of her."

"He's really bright."

The popular herb St John's Wort has a long tradition as a plant that "brightens" mood. Revived in recent years by alternative health product suppliers, legislation that prevents the marketers from making direct medical claims for their product are bypassed by a simple *implied* submodality distinction: "St John's Wort, The *Sunshine* Herb" evokes a bright and positive image. If the tag line were, "It stops you from feeling bleak and miserable," the image evoked would have entirely different submodalities.

Printed on the side of the bright yellow coffee mug given to me by a pharmaceutical firm is a simple childlike drawing of a happy face. The name of the anti-depressant drug that sits happily below it is also printed on the bottom inside of the mug, where you can see it again as you finish your coffee.

Whether by design or intuition, marketers for anti-depressant drugs are also using brightness as a desirable submodality shift. More than one recipient of anti-depressant drugs has suggested that the effect of the drugs was to "brighten them up" or as one of my clients told me, "It made it feel like the sun came out again." I'm left wondering if there is a recursive relationship between brightness and synaptic levels of serotonin. Certainly there seems to be evidence that some depressive disorders can result from low light levels and in recent years "light boxes" have been made commercially available for sufferers of "seasonal affective disorder" who find that a 40-watt light bulb just isn't bright enough for a long winter night.

While on this theme I'd like to mention one great trick passed to me by a hypnosis colleague. While the client is in trance, he slowly raises the brightness of the room with a dimmer switch. If the brightness is increased gradually enough, the client won't notice it. However, they do tend to comment on how everything looks brighter when they open their eyes, and this serves as a convincer that something else has also changed. This trick has the best effect on depressives, especially those who say such things as, "I want you to brighten up my life for me."

It is particularly interesting how often "brightness" is associated with spiritual development, which is often referred to as "enlightenment." While in India, what impressed me about both the Tibetan and Hindu temples were their powerful use of bright colours throughout their decor. Most Christian churches I have dared enter tend to favour dark and drab interiors, illuminated only by rather dark stained glass windows.

In some Western mystical traditions, enlightenment often follows a period of particular difficulty referred to as the "long dark night of the soul." Seekers on the mystical path are often said to be searching for "Illumination." In Kabbalah we have the 8th card of the Major Arcana of "The Hermit" who holds high his shining lamp of wisdom. Delores Ashcroft Nowicki's mystical/occult order is called, "The Servants of the Light," usually abbreviated appropriately enough to "SOL" (as in "solar"—relating to the sun). Of course we cannot leave out the "Illuminati Order" that continues to offer an interesting blend of illumination and paranoia.

Almost invariably, this mysticism and religion intertwine with "after death studies" and there is much anecdotal evidence through the years that suggests that at the edge of life and death, the individual experiences a bright light that brings about a serene and beautiful calm. We also have the Kabbalistic "chakra" of "Tiphereth" located in the *solar plexus* (literally: "sun network"). For Kabbalists, Tiphereth is associated with the "beatific vision" as well as the spiritual illumination of "The Sacrificed Gods." Following the acquisition of the beatific vision, Aleister Crowley wrote:

> I was also granted what mystics describe as "the Beatific Vision" which is the most characteristic of those attributed to Tiphereth, the archetypal idea of beauty and harmony. In this vision one retains one's normal consciousness, but every impression of daily life is as enchanting and exquisite as an ode of Keats. The incidents of life become a harmonious unity; one is lost in a rosy dream of romantic happiness. One may compare it to the effect produced by wine on some people. There is, however, no unreality in the vision. One is not blinded to the facts of existence. It is simply that the normal incoherence and discrepancy between them has been harmonized. (15, p. 777)

Similarly "bright light" seems consistent with the near death experience and religious conversion alike. I have met many evangelical Christians who report that their conversion and Illumination into the mysteries of Christ saved them from the brink of despair/addiction/misery/depression and in a *flash* they achieved a total transformation of their life. It was this consideration of a sudden brightening of internal representation that was fast enough and strong enough to produce such a dramatic shift through threshold that led our hypnosis group to begin experimenting with flashlights.

Since the anaesthetic drug ketamine often produces both out-of-body experiences and near death experiences, I tried to convince one anaesthetic team to join our experiments with the flashlights. We figured that when someone came in for an appendectomy, we could give them a spiritual illumination as part of the deal. Needless to say, the hospital ethics committee wouldn't go for it.

Kenneth Ring (39) classified near death experiences along 4 stages.

1. Feelings of peace and contentment,
2. A sense of detachment from the body,
3. Entering a transitional world of darkness (rapid movements through tunnels: "the tunnel experience"),
4. Emerging into bright light,
5. "Entering the light."

Ketamine is a drug that appears to be able to bring about a similar experience, and in the right circumstances, (dose, set, setting) spiritual transformation. Unlike genuine near death experiences and states induced by the drug DMT, ketamine trips appear to be largely positive affairs, lacking the "heaven or hell" aspects familiar to many psychonauts using other means.

It appears that the drug's effects are brought about by a blockade of brain receptors (drug binding sites) for the neurotransmitter glutamate, producing a flood of glutamate in the brain. While taking the precursor for this transmitter, levo-glutamine, won't have the same effect, I find it interesting that there is a large number of anecdotal reports on the internet of people taking l-glutamine to relieve depression.

A Small Case of Murder

The unfortunate lady sitting before me was a "heart sink" patient, someone who displayed an apparent total inability to connect with anything that might improve her seemingly hopeless life.

My heart actually did sink during the telephone conversation when I answered her message about booking an appointment. Her high expressions of anxiety about treatment, the large number of demands for reassurance, and a shamefully pitiful tone of voice led me to quickly conclude that this lady was a prime candidate for the provocative approach developed by Frank Farrelly. (20)

When she arrived at my office, her eyes had that "mad dog" look of the desperate. Her eyeballs appeared to actually vibrate, and her slumped shoulders and body posture was one of abject helplessness. And that incessantly pathetic tone of voice? Well, it actually started to affect me, and not in a particularly good way. I did start to wonder what effect having to listen to that tonality from the inside— all day and every day—would have on anyone's neurology.

It was clear to me that this was a woman who did not find living very easy. I made some tea and we went over and sat down in my office.

"So Little Miss Anxiety, what can I do for you?" I ask with a smile.

"I don't know. . . . I thought you could help me. Do you think you can help me?" There was that demand for reassurance again. Based on my previous telephone conversation with her, I suspected that I might need to cut through this game straight away. I didn't want to spend the hour trying to win her approval by giving her the right kind of reassurance that she was seeking. So, "Did I think I could help her?"

"Well," I said, "sometimes I get lucky and I can help a client. Other times, I just look at them and think, 'Oh God! If only they didn't fill me with such dread and pity, then I could get them back week after week and get this damned mortgage paid off!' "

She laughed at this and said, "So you think there is hope for me then?"

"Hope?" I laugh, "Not hope, certainly not! What I have here is an opportunity to experiment though, that is sure! As one of my trainers said to me, 'Andy' he said, 'When you find yourself that truly helpless and wretched case, realize that that is your chance to try out all the stuff you've been too scared to try with any other client!— nothing to lose, see!' " She laughed again and visibly relaxed.

"I can see why they told me to come and see you!"

"Ah," I reply, "They probably just know that I'm desperate for clients," which elicited more laughter.

"So," I continued, "What's the problem?" Her state immediately changed as she went back into her trance again, and her face and body posture demonstrated a person who felt serious emotional pain.

"If I tell you what I did, you'll think I am such an awful person." She told me as she struggled to control her weeping.

"Oh no!" I exclaimed, "Not another one!" Throwing my arms in the air and looking upwards as though to address heaven, I say, "Lord, why do you send me these people, . . . the child abusers, the killers, the sodomites, the bastard French. Why, Lord, why? What did I ever do to deserve this?"

I suddenly shift state and look her straight in the eye, point my finger and say in my sternest and fiercest voice, "Look lady, if you are going to tell me that you keep small, underfed and tortured children locked up in your cellar, I'm going straight to the police—do you understand me?"

She changed state again and laughed, "It's not *that* bad," she said.

"Oh here we go again," I say again melodramatically as though to the Lord, "another guilty one trying to make her heinous crimes just sound ordinary!"

I look at her again and ask, "Do you know the reason that most serial killers actually give for killing their victims?" She shook her head and looked at me quizzically.

"Because after all that torture and torment, their victims just get plain annoying, . . ." and I trail off, raising my eyebrows and looking to her expectantly for a response.

"Can I tell you what happened?" She asked as though she was expecting that I wasn't ever going to actually give her the opportunity to do so.

"Go ahead, . . ." I say, in a resigned tone of voice, "but please go easy on me. My nerves are shot to pieces by this line of work. It is no wonder I'm usually so heavily medicated." And I slump back in my chair as though dejected and exhausted.

Briefly her story was this. Her role in life is a rescuer. She has taken in homeless people, distant relatives, and stray cats and dogs. Despite her apparent weakness and vulnerability, it appeared that she had great resolve in assisting other people who were down on their luck and seeing them through the hard times. As Frank Farrelly might say, she is a "national resource." But, one time it went wrong, and it was her reaction to this event that was devastating her.

She had rescued a dog, one that had demonstrated all the signs of an animal that had been horribly abused over a protracted period of time. Two weeks later during a walk in the park, it ran out into the road and was killed by a car.

"So, after just two weeks you got annoyed enough with it to let it be killed?" I proffered. Her face registered both shock and laughter. "I didn't mean for that to happen—" she started to say.

"Oh sure, you didn't *mean* for it to happen. How many prisons the world over are full of 'innocent' people, who are clearly guilty but are claiming, 'I didn't mean for it to happen!' "

"It was just an unfortunate thing. It wasn't—" she protested, but I interrupted her before she could finish.

"—it wasn't *murder*?" I suggested, completing her sentence for her.

"Now look!" she said firmly, but smiling. "It was an accident; the dog got excited and chased a squirrel into the road. I couldn't have known. . . ." She trailed off. Her state changed again, as she slipped back into her trance, and she looked down mournfully. I mirrored her posture and raised my eyebrows to indicate for her to say more.

"It is just so sad that it only had two weeks of a good life before. . . ." she trailed off again.

"You killed it. . . ?"

"You really think it was my fault?" She asked.

"I'm not sure yet," I tell her, "Because there is another possibility. . . ." She looked up at me expectantly. "You have to think about the part that the dog played in all of this. . . . Maybe it was suicide."

She laughed again. An implication here was that the dog, having been abused by its previous owners was so depressed that it committed suicide.

"I mean," I continue, "the poor pooch is sat in the pound, relieved that the traumatic life it had before is over and then. . . Oh, no. . . it gets you! Arrghhhh!" I say with great animation.

She laughed at this and with great emphasis said, "Now listen here, you, I am a good person! I was the best opportunity that poor animal had! It just got excited and chased a squirrel!"

"So," I say, lowering my voice and leaning back and adjusting my posture to that of a "professional" psychotherapist, "What appears to be the problem?"

This sudden change of direction acts as a virtual trance induction. Her eyes glaze over and she becomes very thoughtful for a moment. I've seen this reaction occur when Frank is working. Often the response is "I don't know. . . ." or, "I'm not sure any more. . . ." Sometimes they just look concussed and bewildered.

"You know," she said slowly, "I can't believe I've been so stupid, I've been such a door mat. . . ."

"There you go!" I say quickly, "Insight!"

And on the session went for another 20 minutes in a similar vein. At each step this previously emotionally frail woman became increasingly animated and assertive. Each time she made a negative suggestion about herself I would reframe it into something ludicrous, some kind of resource, or exaggerate it into something far, far worse than it could possibly be. It is worth noting that at no point did I give *any* form of reassurance, or ever attempt to "help" or advise her in any way.

At the 40-minute mark I cut it dead without any attempt to "round it off" or find closure. In true Farrelly style, I smile and ask, "So, did you have any reactions to me in this session?" which of course elicited great laughter. Of course she did have *many* reactions, and these all tumbled forth simultaneously—like a crowd of eager shoppers all trying to get through a narrow doorway at the same time.

One of these was the realisation that she "let people walk all over her" and take advantage of her helpful nature. She highlighted her realisation that although she spent her life helping other people, those people rarely offered anything back, using the resources she offered, and then moving on in their lives when they no longer needed her. She realised that everyone else was moving on except her.

The next 40 minutes were spent discussing, with a fair portion of provocation, her motivation strategies and relationships with other people.

What this session demonstrated so nicely was how the provocative therapy approach forces the client to think outside of her usual patterns. She had had dozens of therapy sessions with a number of different therapists—all without result. I suspect that all her previous therapists had offered help and advice and responded to this lady's extreme prompting for reassurance, thus confirming the reality of her fears.

In a single session lasting approximately 90 minutes from start to finish, this "heart sink" patient and regular attendee to her GP surgery gathered together enough resources to put some major life changes into place. Regular follow-up via telephone over an 8-month period, with 2 short informal meetings demonstrated that these changes continued to develop, evidenced by a marked change in voice tonality, change in appearance, and a quite noticeable playful and flirtatious manner.

Missionary Zeal

*"The belief that one's own view of reality is the only reality is
the most dangerous of all delusions. It becomes still more
dangerous if it is coupled with a missionary zeal
to enlighten the rest of the world, whether the rest
of the world wishes to be enlightened or not."*
—Paul Watzlawick

When I was very small, a relative showed me a trick with an
apple tree and a bottle. In spring when an apple on the tree is still
very small, a bottle is placed over the apple and tied to the branch.
The apple then grows inside the bottle. When picked from the tree
later, it becomes a mystery as to how the full-sized apple got inside
the bottle.

It was with this in mind that I encountered my first ethical
dilemma. Exploring some tidepools as a child, I found an old sub-
merged bottle. Inside was a crab that was far too big to get out of the
bottle. I immediately understood how it got there, but was confused
as to my responsibilities. If I left the crab to its imprisonment, it
would remain safe but severely limited. If I set it free, then while it
might have its freedom, it might also lack the skills to survive. It
seemed that whatever I did would have negative consequences, yet
to simply walk away seemed to be a neglect of duty.

This is a dilemma that faces many therapists and NLP practitioners, and is a source of much frustration. They can see the simple
changes that someone else—not a paying client—needs to make in
order to improve their life, but the person cannot see it. It isn't entirely
uncommon for the NLP practitioner to initially annoy every friend,
colleague and acquaintance they meet, because of his or her ambition
to change the world and make everyone in it happier. When I meet
life coaches, NLPers, counsellors, and therapists socially, I sometimes

I find their enthusiasm intrusive and, quite frankly, rude. I rarely meet psychiatrists in social situations who are so passionate about their work that they want to madicate me or anyone else they meet.

Recently in an NLP practice group, one very strange lady— clearly the recipient of far too much training—interrupted a conversation I was having with a friend, and demanded in an arrogant tonality that I show her my "peak state." "Excuse me?" I asked, somewhat taken aback. She continued, "If you think you are so good, then show me your peak state!" Afterward, I realised that the most useful response might have been to ask gently, "Is this *your* peak state?" The response she actually received was possibly far ruder than necessary, but at least she got the point—she went away and left me alone.

There seems to be an expectation with some NLP practitioners that they need to live in a peak state all the time, and I watch them at conferences and seminars struggling so hard to do so. I often think of these lost souls as wandering the earth like extras from *Village Of The Damned,* or *The Stepford Wives*—quite out of touch with normality and frightening all the "normals" they meet. If this is you, please stop it. If I am a crab in a bottle, please remember that it is my bottle, not yours.

Sometimes it is not so much what you can *do* that will bring about the biggest change, but who you can *be*. The very best role models, to whom others aspire, rarely interfere directly with other people's lives—they live their own lives and *be* the best they can be.

The doors to the future are wide open, and the opportunities are endless. There are many things today that we take for granted that only a few decades ago would have been unimaginable. Recorded music, clean water, the internet, space travel, mobile telephones, life extension, more and more cures for previously fatal or life-threatening disease, the list is endless. What are we currently not even imagining that future generations will take for granted in future years?

The same is true of our internal lives. Only a few of us are able to live out our lives in ways that are truly satisfying, and able to see how we are stuck in a bottle and how to get out of it. Our collective imagination hasn't reached its outer limit.

At least not yet.

Footprints

I encountered my first dying patient when I was 18 and working on a general surgical ward. It was a beautiful summer day—not too hot, just perfect. It was a Sunday and the ward was quiet.

Thomas, a 24-year-old, had undergone major surgery, was about to die, and knew it. The surgical treatment he had undergone had been performed with the best of intentions, but unfortunately the complications that arose from it only served to accelerate his demise. He was quite philosophical about it, and didn't hold any resentment. "I've left enough footprints" he told me, "I can pick up the trail again next time around."

He had only one desire and that was to be taken outside into the shade provided by a large oak tree nearby. "I want to die outside, under that tree," he told me.

Well, I could see no problem with that, so his parents and girlfriend and I began to wheel his bed outside.

It didn't take long before our path was blocked by a ferocious looking Ward Sister and some nurses whose expressions told me that this wasn't going to be pretty.

"Where do you think you are going?" The Sister barked.

"Outside. . . " I said nervously.

". . . to die!" added Thomas calmly.

"Put this man back where he is supposed to be!" the Sister commanded the other nurses. I was ordered to go and wait in the office and contemplate my behaviour.

The character assassination and interrogation as to "just what was I thinking?" took about 20 minutes. I learned that rules had to be obeyed and professionalism was to be adhered to at all times. Patients were not allowed to go outside willy-nilly just to go and die under trees. This was simply not acceptable—there are rules about these things.

While I was in the office receiving this wisdom, Thomas died. During those same 20 minutes a great number of changes began to occur in me.

One was a robust disrespect for bureaucratic rules.

And another was to live by Thomas's simple philosophy and "Leave enough footprints."

This book is one of them.

Appendix
A Primer on Submodalities

"The lions in Trafalgar Square could have been eagles or bulldogs and still have carried the same (or similar) message about Empire and about the cultural premises of nineteenth century England. And yet, how different might their message have been had they been made of wood!"
—Gregory Bateson (10, p. 130)

In the early stages of NLP, one of the key understandings that opened up a host of possibilities for changing someone's experience was the realization that any (and every) experience is made up of representations in one or more of the five sensory modalities: vision, hearing, feeling, (and usually to a lesser degree) taste and smell. This is true even when someone is using abstract verbal descriptions that follow the rigorous formal rules of symbolic logic. At some point, those statements refer to sensory-based experience (visual, auditory, kinaesthetic, olfactory or gustatory).

This realization made it possible, for instance, to change someone's feeling response to a particular sight or sound, without changing the content of the sight or sound itself. The five modalities are the larger building blocks of experience; changing one or more of these components is much easier than trying to change the entire experience all at once.

Submodalities are the smaller components *within* each modality. For instance, any internal visual image will have a certain size, brightness, clarity, focus, distance from the viewer, location in space, etc. Every sound will have a certain tone, tempo, volume and location, etc. Every kinaesthetic experience will have a certain extent, location, temperature, pressure, etc.

These are called *analogue* submodalities, because they can vary continuously over a range. For instance, the size of an image can vary from a tiny speck to larger than the known universe. The brightness of an image can vary from so dark you can't see what is there, to an intensity that is so great all you can see is white light. The volume of a sound can vary from barely detectable to ear-splitting, and the tone can vary continuously across the scale of audible frequencies. The extent of a kinaesthetic experience can vary from a single point to the entire surface of your body, and temperature can vary from very cold to extremely hot.

Other submodalities function in a digital "either/or" way. An image can be black and white *or* colour, still *or* moving, flat *or* three-dimensional—but not both at once. Within one half of a digital either/ or submodality there is usually an analogue range. For instance, a colourful image can vary from a very pale pastel to very bright saturated colours, and a moving image can vary from very slow-motion to a fast-forward blur. These elements within the modalities are easier to change than the entire modality, making it easier and simpler to teach someone how to change their experience when it is unsatisfactory.

However, before you can change the submodalities of an experience, you have to know what they are to begin with. One way to do this is to ask someone simple questions like, "Is that image that terrifies you moving or still, close or far, colour or black and white," etc. However, sometimes that isn't necessary, because the submodalities of someone's experience are often expressed in their language, usually quite unconsciously.

Distance
There are many references to distance in ordinary conversation, for instance:
"That was too close for comfort."
"It all seems so far away now."
"It was a close call."
"I need some personal space."
"I just want to run away from it."
"She's always 'in my face.' "
"I need to get some distance from my problems."
"I want to take a step back from it all."
"Why won't you let me get close to you?"

The last example is an interesting one. One person in a relationship wants more closeness than the other, who may feel "smothered," possibly the exact difficulty presented by, and to, people with autism. Oliver Sacks (41) reports that distance or proximity is a powerful force in people with Tourette's syndrome—on one occasion, eating in a restaurant with three Touretters, each needed to sit in the corner, lest another diner sit too close behind them.

Distance is a powerful real-world solution to a great many problems, so it's not surprising that it is often effective in our inner world as well. When faced with a nasty-looking tiger that is getting rapidly closer, fear will increase with proximity, and a feeling of security and calm is only likely to be achieved once maximum distance is achieved. Similarly, on an African plain, a lion in the far distance is unlikely to raise too much concern—until it turns and starts running in your direction. Many mothers advise their children to "stay away" from certain people, and bystanders are told to "stand back" for their safety. There are very few immediate real-world problems that a sufficient distance won't cure, although the consequences may be problematic. The unfortunate outcome of this effect can sometimes be a generalised "away from" meta-program where someone might always "run away from" their problems. But then as Snoopy once said, "There is no problem so big that it cannot be run away from."

Take a minute or two now to pick some memory and experiment with changing the distance between you and that image over a wide range, to experience how that changes your response to it.

Colour

"Colourful" expressions occur frequently in everyday language, and they often indicate the emotional feeling responses that people have to an experience.

"He makes me green with envy."

"She was tickled pink."

"I'm feeling blue."

"A black comedy."

"He's a colourful character."

"That made me see red."

One rather pale and drawn client arrived in my office, dressed in clothes that were all either grey or black, and she spoke in a flat, toneless voice. After the preliminaries, I asked, "What can I do for you today?"

Her reply was simple enough, and very direct and explicit: "I want you to put some colour into my life." When I asked her about the submodalities of her visual representations, they were universally coded in black and white—no matter what the content.

Pause to pick some anticipated future event and experiment with your image of it, varying from no colour at all to vibrant saturated colours, and notice how that affects your response to it.

Size

Size is a common part of many expressions, and is particularly evident in young children, who are particularly sensitive to their small size in relation to enormous adults.

"It's all gotten blown out of proportion."
"He shrinks from success."
"It's no big deal."
"I've walked tall since I got that promotion."
"I'll cut him down to size."
"Sizing up an opportunity."
"He takes up a lot of space."
"When I approached him, I felt like I was two inches tall."

One interesting thing I've heard a lot recently from the DJ culture is how a submodality distinction becomes the digital communication itself, such as, "And now we have a 'big shout out' to all our fans out there," "Giving it large," "larging it up," etc.

Stop now to think of some situation in which you are relating to someone else with greater or lesser authority or importance, and notice how large you are in relation to that other person. Then change that relationship by making either yourself or that other person larger or smaller, and notice how that changes your response to them.

Movement

Someone's experience of movement (or lack of it) is often reflected in their language.

"It all happened so quickly it was just a blur."
"Time seems to drag."
"Time stopped."

"Slow down, will you; I can't keep up."

"I was frozen in place.

"He's slow-witted."

"Now stop and think for a moment."

Movement within visual representations will strongly influence your experience of time. Decision strategies are also strongly affected; an impulsive person often uses still images, so the consequences and outcomes are deleted from their decision process, and they often repeat the same bad decisions. Others decide based on extensive movies that allow them to think things through to their inevitable conclusion and see the consequences.

Zihl, von Cramon and Mai (46) have identified a specific set of cells adjacent to the V4 area of the visual cortex that are involved specifically in processing of motion.

> The visual disorder complained of by the patient was a loss of movement in all three dimensions. She had difficulty, for example, in pouring tea or coffee into a cup because the fluid appeared frozen, like a glacier. In addition, she could not stop pouring at the right time since she was unable to perceive the movement in the cup (or a pot) as the fluid rose. . . . In a room where more than two other people were walking, she felt very insecure and unwell, and usually left the room immediately, because "People were suddenly here or there but I have not seen them moving." . . . She could not cross the street because of her inability to judge the speed of a car, but she could identify the car itself without difficulty. . . . She gradually learned to "estimate" the distance of moving vehicles by means of the sound becoming louder. (46, p. 315)

Think of a pleasant memory and first notice whether your image of it is a movie or a still picture. Then experiment with changing it from a still to a movie (or vice versa) and then vary the speed of the movie, from slow motion to fast forward, and notice how that changes your response to it. Your response will vary somewhat with content, so try several different experiences, and try something unpleasant, too.

Association/Disassociation

Association is being *inside* an experience, in contrast to watching an event from the *outside*. Sometimes someone will say things like, "It was just like it was happening again," an indication of association, or "I can see myself doing that," an indication of dissociation. At other times other cues will be more useful. Someone who is associated typically moves more, in an expressive and animated way that is congruent with the activity or event that they are thinking about, while someone who is dissociated will move much less, and may even be quite still.

"I just don't see myself as the sort of person who would really enjoy doing that." Of course, those familiar with the meta-model might be tempted to ask, "Well, just what *do* you see yourself doing?" but before we go there, let's just take a look at something described by Richard Bandler.

When doing a Swish pattern (2, ch. 3; 7, ch. 1) to change behaviour (for instance to increase motivation), we swish from an *associated* position (in a context that inhibits motivation) and we swish toward a *dissociated* representation of yourself being motivated. The initial associated position includes representations of the context in which the change is desired, connecting the cues in the imagined context to the new behaviour. Then when the real world cues are experienced, they trigger the behavioural change.

There are also less useful ways to use the same process. I regularly encounter medical students who are afraid of that great institution, the viva—the oral examination that is the trial by fire of medical students everywhere. What I hear is, "I just see myself standing there and feeling nervous, and everyone just staring at me, and I just screw it all up." The repeated word "just" ensures that they can't pay attention to anything else. If they are doing this really well, here's how they do it:

Create a dissociated movie out there in the future time line, and make it one that gradually slows down the longer it goes on. Each day, the movie gets one day closer, and proportionally bigger. As it gets bigger, the focus becomes clearer, so more detail becomes apparent.

As each day passes and the movie gets proportionally closer and larger, the feelings of anxiety increase proportionally. Day by day, the student watches the movie over and over again, seeing themselves screwing it all up and feeling really bad about it. As they watch it over and over again, they are perfectly training their neurology, teaching it exactly what do when the real world trigger tells them it's time.

Eventually, when the day arrives, they stand there on the stage for real, and having rehearsed it so many times by now, *they screw it up perfectly*—precisely as they rehearsed it so many times.

I like to tease students with the most basic of questions, yet one that seems to confuse so many: "What do the swish pattern (described above), and the double dissociation pattern have in common?"

The answer, of course, is that both have submodality changes, and both use association and dissociation, but in different ways. For example, let's take the standard "see yourself in a cinema" double dissociation phobia cure pattern from a submodality perspective.

"Find yourself sitting comfortably in a cinema, notice how far away the cinema screen is, who is sitting to your left, who is sitting to your right, etc." (This creates association into the experience of being in a cinema, and dissociation from anything that might appear on the movie screen. Being in a cinema also implies observing something that is not real, in perfect safety.) "Now float up out of your body and into the projection room." This creates association into the context of the projection room, and dissociation from being in the cinema, a further separation from whatever might appear on the screen.

"Place your hands on the plexiglass window at the front of the projection room" occupies the kinaesthetic modality, while presupposing an impenetrable separation between what is inside the room and what is viewed through the window.

"So you can watch yourself sitting in the cinema, watching the screen." The observer in the projection booth observes the self in the cinema, who is observing the movie screen, a double dissociation.

"Now run the movie of yourself having the phobic response on the screen in black and white, from beginning to end." The phobic response is now seen as a black and white, framed, flat, distant movie, contextualised within the cinema itself and all the implications of that context. The "from beginning to end" piece is also important, because often a phobic will experience it as "endless"— either as a still image, or as a loop that repeats over and over.

Try this process yourself to experience the lessening of feelings that results from dissociation, and which is so useful in changing the intensely unpleasant feelings in response to phobias, PTSD and other traumatic memories. *But be warned:* the same thing will happen if you dissociate from a pleasant memory, and in that case you would lose access to those resourceful feelings. Of course this could be useful if those pleasant memories compulsively lead you into an addictive behaviour with harmful consequences.

The sound in movies typically comes from near the movie screen, rather than from all around us as it does in the real world, and this supports the dissociation created by the flat visual image on the distant screen. While many of us are waiting for the technology driving virtual reality to give us total immersion and association into the events portrayed, interesting experiences can be found at the local cinema with Dolby™ surround sound. As a good trance subject, I have often found myself ducking from bullets that sound like they are flying over my head and rather amusingly really did "hit the deck" as ordered by the sergeant on the screen as a screaming grenade flew in nearby.

The double dissociation is simply a process, or an activity (some would say a story) that the client can follow, and which creates all the submodality changes required in order for them to change their state and have a more comfortable and resourceful response. The exact nature of the activity/story that we construct for the client really isn't all that important, as long as it has the appropriate submodality structure.

In his book, "Therapeutic Metaphors" (24) David Gordon elucidates the strategies useful for influencing submodalities through storytelling. I found this methodology particularly helpful when working on a children's oncology unit, where the majority of patients seemed to be 6-year-olds suffering from leukaemia. Naturally, given the nature of children, very few of them followed the rules by which medicine views how people with leukaemia should behave, and very soon I found myself being called upon to read stories at three o'clock in the morning. One problem with gaining a reputation as a good storyteller is that pretty soon *every* child in the vicinity demands a story—and some adults will also want theirs.

Following an ear piercing accident involving too much sambuca, a nail gun and an embarrassing display of macho exuberance in Cape Town, South Africa, I remembered the old technique for pain control

whereby you see yourself in the mirror, an easy way to create dissociation. It's a neat trick, because explaining the difference between
association and dissociation might be too abstract and complicated
for some clients, but "Look in the mirror" is easy to follow. As a colleague points out, seeing yourself in the mirror doesn't really mean
that you are dissociated, because you are inside an associated picture
seeing a picture of yourself dissociated. However, the more you
attend to the qualities and detail in that mirror-image, the less you
will attend to the painful feelings in your body. Seeing myself in a
mirror certainly reduced the pain in the absence of further sambuca.

Frame/Panoramic

Real world experiences are panoramic; they occur all around
you in three-dmensional space. But when an image is framed, it
exists in a particular location, and at a certain distance from the
viewer. And since very few framed images are 3-D, framing an image
tends to make it flat. Seeing yourself in a mirror also includes a frame
(unless it's an improbable panoramic mirror!), so the content and
context of a frame also affects the submodalities. We can increase
distance by suggesting that they see themselves in the mirror while
standing on the other side of the room, and of course this distance
will also reduce the size of the image.

Probably these days people are more likely to make their internal images in frames because they are so familiar with seeing them
that way on a television set or cinema screen. Putting a frame around
a picture will have several effects; the principal one is that it presupposes dissociation.

While contemporary cinema cannot yet do away with the frame
that contains the projection, one movie did a pretty good job of it for
many people. The much-hyped movie, "The Blair Witch Project"
showed every scene filmed from a first person perspective. So, with
four actors in the movie, the viewer could see only a maximum of
three of them at any time. At the screening I attended, more than one
person managed to suspend reality long enough to forget that they
were really sitting in a cinema rather than irretrievably lost a forest
full of dangers.

This effect of immersion into projected events are best captured
by the "space rides" offered at some fairs, where the patrons sit inside

a space ship facing the front "window" which is actually a projection of a high speed space chase filmed in the first person perspective. The problem of the frame around the screen and dissociation are overcome by making them part of the environment of the projection and illusion—*the frame becomes part of the event experienced.* In some pornography and film noir, this contextualisation of the frame is achieved by the "viewer as voyeur" technique, where the frame itself coincides with a window or doorway through which the events are witnessed. There is also the "unsteady camera" technique much used in the popular TV drama "NYPD Blue" to create the illusion of participating in the scene as a "fly on the wall" or even as the person holding the camera itself. It was interesting that the cult reality TV show, "Big Brother," exceptionally popular with the internet generation, was presented in an interactive (hence associated) internet type format.

As far as NLPers are concerned, this clever adaptation by our TV and movie producers is likely to influence the referential structures we use in our change work. Imagine a generation that has grown up where two-dimensionally projected entertainment mediums no longer exist. This is the generation for whom a "night-in" involves entering a virtual reality room where all imagery is associated, 3-D and interactive. They get to both shoot up the bad guys *and* bed the heroine/hero. In this generation the slow motion and pause buttons may see a great deal of use. But will this be the generation that has no reference experience for dissociation from a two-dimensional framed picture?

Summary

All the foregoing relies on the fact that our inner world is mostly parallel to the outer world. For example, we described earlier how distance and the feeling of safety are proportional to each other and also how distance and size are proportional. Other than smoke there are very few events in the natural world that get bigger as they go further away, and there are no naturally-occurring events that get proportionally louder as you see them move further away. As yet we have no moving thing that creates an inverse Doppler effect—something that sounds as if it is moving away from us, while we see it moving toward us. Submodalities fit together in expected and familiar relationships, and we can use these relationships to alter someone's internal experience, changing their response to external events.

When people *do* have experiences that violate these familiar relationships, they are quite striking and puzzling. If they are not easily explained by fever or having taken some drug, they are often attributed to paranormal influences or given a religious significance. For instance, a startling effect can be experienced when driving through a short tunnel where you can see what is on the other side of the tunnel, or along a straight tree-lined road with a distant mountain seen between the trees. The distant image will appear to get smaller as we approach it, rather than larger, because they don't increase in size as rapidly as the tunnel or trees. Similar effects are utilised by film editors when the camera simultaneously pans back while zooming in on the subject.

Submodality changes can be used directly to help people change their experience, and when they make changes in other ways, shifts in their submodalities can teach us how that occurred.

About the Author

Formerly a registered nurse working in clinical neurology and neurosurgery, Andrew T. Austin began his nursing career in Accident and Emergency, where he quickly developed a strong reputation for working with the many psychiatric and mental health-related emergencies that were frequently presented to the department. It was during this period in 1994 that he began training in hypnosis and therapy, and his interest in psychotherapy and neurolinguistics grew.

Andrew organises The West Sussex Hypnosis and NLP Study Group where he currently is focusing on neurology and the treatment of clinical conditions.

Via his frequent writings, workshops, and lectures Andrew T. Austin is rapidly becoming known as the leading NLP-oriented therapist emphasising the neurological aspects of personal change and therapy. His seminars and workshops are sought out by NLP practitioners, trainers, and psychotherapists seeking to deepen their knowledge and skills base of the neurological underpinnings of their work. He lives in the south of England. Contact: nlp@hotmail.co.uk

Bibliography

1. Andreas, Connirae; and Andreas, Steve. *Heart of The Mind: engaging your inner power to change with neuro-linguistic programming.* Boulder, CO, Real People Press, 1989

2. Andreas, Connirae; and Andreas, Steve. *Change Your Mind—and Keep the Change.* Boulder, CO, Real People Press, 1987

3. Andreas, Connirae; and Andreas, Tamara. *Core Transformation: reaching the wellspring within.* Boulder, CO, Real People Press, 1994

Andreas, Tamara. *Core Transformation—the Full 3-Day Workshop.* DVD program. Boulder, CO, Real People Press, 2007

4. Andreas, Steve. *Virginia Satir: the patterns of her magic.* Boulder, CO, Real People Press, 1991

5. Andreas, Steve. "Resolving Grief." http://www.steveandreas.com/grief02.html 2002

6. Bandler, Richard. *Time for a Change.* Cupertino, CA, Meta Publications, 1993

7. Bandler, Richard. *Magic in Action.* Cupertino CA. Meta Publications, 1984

8. Bandler, Richard; and Grinder, John. *Reframing: neuro-linguistic programming and the transformation of meaning.* Boulder, CO, Real People Press, 1982

9. Bandler, Richard; and Grinder, John. *Frogs into Princes: neuro-linguistic programming.* Boulder, CO, Real People Press, 1979

10. Bateson, Gregory. *Steps to an Ecology of Mind: Collected Essays in Anthropology, Psychiatry, Evolution, and Epistemology.* Chicago IL, University of Chicago Press, 2000

11. Bateson, Gregory; and Ruesch, Jurgen. *Communication: The Social Matrix of Psychiatry* New York, W. W. Norton & Company, 1951

12. Bourland, David; and Dennithorn Johnston, Paul. *To Be or Not: An E-Prime Anthology.* Concord, CA, International Society for General Semantics, 1991

13. Campbell, Frank; and Singer, George. *Brain and Behaviour.* Headington Hill Hall, Oxford, Pergamon Press, 1979

14. Carter, Rita. *Mapping The Mind*. Berkeley, CA, University of California Press, 1999

15. Crowley, Aleister. *The Confessions of Aleister Crowley* New York, Arkana Publishing, 1979

16. Cytowic, Richard E. *The Man Who Tasted Shapes*. Cambridge, MA, MIT Press, 1998

17. Deveson, Anne. *Tell Me I'm Here: one family's experience of schizophrenia*. London, Penguin Books, 1998

18. *Diagnostic and Statistical Manual of Mental Disorders DSM-IV-TR* Fourth Edition. Arlington VA, American Psychiatric Association. 2000

19. Dilts, Robert. *Sleight of Mouth: the magic of conversational belief Change*. Cupertino, CA, Meta Publications, 2006

20. Farrelly, Frank; and Brandsma, Jeff. *Provocative Therapy*. Cupertino, CA, Meta Publications, 1974

21. Frankl, Victor. *Man's Search for Meaning: an introduction to Logotherapy*. New York, Washington Square Books, 1984

22. Goffman, Erving. *Stigma: notes on the management of spoiled identity*. New York, Simon and Schuster, 1986

23. Goffman, Erving. *Asylums: essays on the social situation of mental patients and other inmates*. New York, Anchor Books, 1961

24. Gordon, David. *Therapeutic Metaphors: Helping Others Through The Looking Glass*. Cupertino, CA, Meta Publications, 1978

25. Haley, Jay. *Strategies of Psychotherapy*. New York, Grune & Stratton, 1963

26. Kesey, Ken. *One Flew over the Cuckoo's Nest*. London, Penguin Books, 1977

27. Laing, R. D. *The Politics of the Family*. New York, Routledge, 1998

28. Laing, R. D. *Wisdom, Madness and Folly: the making of a psychiatrist*. London, MacMillan, 1985

29. Laing, R.D. *The Politics of Experience and the Bird of Paradise*. London, Penguin Books, 1968

30. Laing, R.D. *The Divided Self: An Existential Study in Sanity and Madness*. London, Penguin Books, 1965

31. Laing, R. D. *Sanity,Madness, and the Family*. London, Tavistock, 1964

32. Laing, R. D. *Self and Others*. London, Tavistock Publications, 1961

33. Ornstein, Robert. *The Right Mind: making sense of the hemispheres*. New York, Harcourt, 1997

34. Pendergrast, Mark. *Victims of Memory: Sex Abuse Accusations and Shattered Lives*. Hinesburg VT, Upper Access, 1996

35. Perls, Fritz. *Gestalt Therapy Verbatim*. Highland, NY, Gestalt Journal Press, 1968

36. Ramachandran, Vilaynur; and Blakeslee, Sandra. Phantoms in the Brain: probing the mysteries of the human mind. New York, Harpercollins, 1999

37. Reps, Paul. Zen Flesh, Zen Bones: a collection of Zen and pre-Zen writings. New York, Doubleday Anchor Books, 1976

38. Ridley, Matt. *The Red Queen: sex and the evolution of human nature*. New York, MacMillan, 1993

39. Ring, K. *Life at Death*. New York, Coward McCann, 1980

40. Rosenhan, David, L. "On Being Sane in Insane Places." Science, vol. 179, pp. 250-258, Jan. 1973

41. Sacks, Oliver. *An Anthropologist on Mars: seven paradoxical tales*. New York, Random House, 1996

42. Schacter, Stanley; & Rodin, Judith. *Obese Humans and Rats*. Hoboken, N.J., John Wiley and Sons, 1974

43. Siebert, Al, Ph.D. "How Non-Diagnostic Listening Led to a Rapid 'Recovery' from Paranoid Schizophrenia." Excerpted from *Journal of Humanistic Psychology*, vol. 40, No. 1, pp. 34-58, Winter, 2000. http://www.successfulschizophrenia.org

44. Watzlawick, Paul; Beavin, Janet Helmick; and Jackson, Don D. *Pragmatics of Human Communication: study of interactional patterns, pathologies and paradoxes*. New York, W. W. Norton, 1967

45. Wilson, Robert Anton, *Coincidance*. Tempe, AZ, New Falcon Publications, 1991

46. Zihl, J., von Cramon, D., & Mai, N. "Selective disturbance of movement vision after bilateral brain damage." *Brain*, vol. 106, pp. 313-340, 1983

Index